'Spreadsheet Check and Control **does what no other book before has attempted to do**; provide standards for designing spreadsheets that lend themselves to a logical review by management and internal auditors. Following this author's guide and insight can help your organization minimize spreadsheet errors and facilitate audit review to prevent and detect those errors.' Jim Kaplan, AuditNet.org.

'It is **excellent**. I am embarrassed when I think of the shortcuts I generally take with spreadsheets and I have often paid the price. I think it will become, and it should be, **required reading** for all young trainee accountants.' Ciaran Walsh, senior finance specialist, Irish Management Institute.

'It's **super**. I kept saying to myself, "Wow, I didn't know you could do that." A **great job**.' Ray Panko, University of Hawai'i.

'Patrick O'Beirne's *Spreadsheet Check and Control* is the kind of serendipitous book that only comes along once in a great while. I thought I knew a lot about Excel, but in the course of teaching me to be Excel-careful, O'Beirne taught me some **new tricks and methods** that both helped me build **better financial models** and track down errors.' Simon Benninga, author of Financial Modeling, MIT Press 2000 and Principles of Finance with Excel, Oxford University Press, 2005.

'Save red faces all round by **buying, absorbing and passing-on this book**, especially if you personally develop spreadsheets or if your organization is subject to Sarbanes Oxley and related regulations. Avoiding even a trivial spreadsheet mistake may well pay for the book. Avoiding a large one may **save your career**.' Dr. Gary Hinson, independent consultant in information security and computer auditing, editor of security awareness website NoticeBored.com.

'Probably one of the **most important spreadsheet books** ever written. Your customers and boss will be delighted with the increased usability, accuracy and reliability his techniques encourage. Be aware that the pages are **packed** with useful and usable advice, so the 200 pages is probably equivalent to 500 pages in many other books.' Simon Murphy, Codematic.net, author of XLAnalyst.

Spreadsheet Check and Control

47 key practices to detect and prevent errors

Patrick O'Beirne

First Edition

Systems Publishing, Tara Hill, Gorey, Co. Wexford, Ireland

Spreadsheet Check and Control: 47 key practices to detect and prevent errors

by Patrick O'Beirne.

ISBN 1-905404-00-X

Published by Systems Publishing, Villa Alba, Tara Hill, Gorey, Co. Wexford, IRELAND

Tel: +353 (0)55 22294   Fax: +353 (0)55 22165

E-mail: SP@SystemsPublishing.com

URL: http://www.SystemsPublishing.com

Copyright © 2005 Systems Publishing.

Attention Businesses, Training companies, and Conference Organisers:

The publisher offers this book at bulk discounts for use as training courseware, promotional materials, prizes or gifts.

A catalogue record for this book is available from the British Library.

Cover design: Bennis Design. Editor: Alex Miller.

Microsoft and Excel are trademarks of Microsoft Corporation. Extracts from the Microsoft Help files have been quoted by permission of Microsoft Corporation.

The example companies, organisations, products, domain names, email addresses, logos, people, places and events depicted herein are fictitious. No association with any real company, organisation, product, domain name, email address, logo, person, place or event is intended or should be inferred.

Systems Publishing is a registered business name of Systems Modelling Limited, registered in Ireland no. 84616, web site http://www.sysmod.com

To my wife, Megan, in gratitude for her constant support and encouragement.

Acknowledgements

I thank everyone who made this book possible. Special thanks are due to the founders of the European Spreadsheet Risk Interest Group (Eusprig) – David Chadwick of the University of Greenwich, Pat Cleary of the University of Wales in Cardiff, and Ray Butler of HM Customs & Excise. They started Eusprig in 2000, following on pioneering research by Ray Panko in Hawaii.

Garry Cleere, Aidan Perdisatt, Graham Macdonald, Grenville Croll and Louise Pryor have all contributed generously with their reviews and comments.

I also thank all the experts and gurus in the spreadsheet world who contributed by participating freely in the Excel-L list, who provide helpful tips on their websites, and who provided me with evaluation copies of their spreadsheet auditing software.

And to you, the reader, it could not have been possible without the belief that you wanted it! I wish you every success in mastering the challenge of spreadsheet control.

Introduction

Are your spreadsheets important? This book is for you! It describes good practices that all spreadsheet users should follow.

Use this book to learn how to avoid the most common errors and to make future development easier. If you are a software tester or a manager of end-user-computing, it gives you techniques for checking spreadsheets for accuracy and soundness. If you are an auditor looking for evidence of fraud, such as deliberately concealed data or functionality, you will also benefit from knowing the many ways in which data can be hidden or calculation methods subverted.

To derive the fullest benefit from this book, you should already have spreadsheet skills corresponding to the European Computer Driving Licence (ECDL) Module 4 (M4) or Advanced Module 4 (AM4). The focus of this book is on spreadsheet construction using formulas. All the examples are in Microsoft Excel. They have been tested in Excel versions 97, 2000, 2002(XP), and 2003. We mention a few differences between Excel 97 and Excel 2002/2003.

Why is this book necessary?

This book was created in response to expressions of concerns by managers about risk to the business from a pervasive dependence on spreadsheets. Barry Boehm, in his article 'Software Defect Reduction Top 10 List' [1] warned: 'The ranks of *sorcerer's apprentice* user-programmers will swell rapidly, giving many who have little training or expertise in how to avoid or detect high-risk defects tremendous power to create high-risk defects'. He proposed that to help reduce the likelihood of user errors, developers should provide the equivalent of seat belts and air bags in cars, along with safe-driving aids and rules of the road. This fits in nicely with the 'Driving Licence' analogy!

---

[1] www.cebase.org/www/News/top-10-defects.html Boehm, B. and Basili, V. R. (2001, January). "Software Defect Reduction Top 10," Computer, 135-137.

Regulators are examining spreadsheet controls

The UK HM Revenue and Customs department audit the tax returns for Value-Added Tax (VAT) submitted to them in spreadsheet form. The largest VAT error found in a spreadsheet in 2001 was around £1M sterling (about €1.5M, or $1.9M). Recovering that amount gave them a very good payback on their investment in developing spreadsheet auditing software and skills.

The US Food and Drug Administration (FDA) have rigorous specifications for the integrity of electronic records. These include spreadsheets used as laboratory log books.

The US Sarbanes-Oxley Act requires auditors to comment on internal controls over financial reporting. As consolidation and reporting is frequently done by spreadsheets, management are spending more time on review and testing.

The European Spreadsheet Risk Interest Group

The European Spreadsheet Risks Interest Group (Eusprig) publish research on spreadsheet errors on their website `www.eusprig.org`. Their annual conference attracts speakers from all over the world to present on tools and techniques for the detection, correction, and prevention of spreadsheet errors.

Researchers from ISACA (Northern UK Chapter), University of Wales Institute Cardiff and the University of Greenwich met in 1999 to discuss the ever-increasing problem of business risk associated with spreadsheet errors. As a result of this meeting they founded Eusprig. This group aims to increase awareness of spreadsheet risk among academia and industry. It also promotes research into the extent and nature of the problem, methods of preventing and detecting of errors and methods of limiting damage. This has brought together researchers and professionals in the areas of business, software engineering and auditing to seek effective solutions. It now includes interested parties from HM Revenue and Customs, PricewaterhouseCoopers, KPMG, the British Computer Society (BCS), the Dutch Computer Society (NGI) and the Netherlands Bank, as well as many other companies and individuals.

The ECDL Foundation

The European Computer Driving Licence (ECDL) foundation in Dublin, Ireland, develops the ECDL syllabus for the certification of users in computer competence. They found demand from companies for certification, beyond technical knowledge, to include a level of self-awareness and responsibility for data integrity and calculation correctness. Accordingly, in 2003 they met with experts in the European Spreadsheet Risk Interest Group (Eusprig) to capture current best practices in design quality and the avoidance of errors. They presented a paper at the fifth Eusprig conference[2] in Klagenfurt, Austria, in 2004. In it, they outlined their goals for a future syllabus:

> [This] Module requires the candidate to appreciate their responsibility for good spreadsheet design and use given the scope and significance of spreadsheets use in the contemporary workplace. The candidate shall appreciate the need for good spreadsheets specification, be aware of some of the key security considerations, and appreciate the benefits of clearly organised, well presented and easy-to-use spreadsheets. The candidate shall be able to construct sound spreadsheets, find and correct common errors, and test for input and output accuracy. It is anticipated that the candidate will already have mastered the skills and achieved the knowledge detailed in ECDL Module 4, Spreadsheets, or ECDL Module AM4, Spreadsheets, Advanced-Level.

---

[2] http://www.isys.uni-klu.ac.at/ISYS/eusprig04/

The structure of this book

Each section is organised as follows:

> The key practice item appears in a heavy box.

The item is followed by some *definitions* of any special terms that are used.

This is followed by a description of the essential skills needed, and examples.

> Stories with web links in a shaded box give reported cases of expensive mistakes that have been made by not following good practice.

Each section ends with a 'Check your knowledge' self-test marked with a *writing hand* symbol in the left margin. The answers are in the back of the book. Most exercises use sample files that you download from http://www.sysmod.com/sbp. You may be asked for a username and password taken from a page of this book.

Typographical conventions

Normal text appears in a normal typeface.

Worksheet names and special terms are shown *in italics*.

Spreadsheet file names are shown in **boldface**.

`Code samples and formulas appear in monospace text.`

Microsoft Excel Menu commands and dialog text appear in sans serif text.

The > symbol means you continue to a submenu or dialog tab, eg <u>F</u>ile > <u>O</u>pen. The underlined letters indicate where shortcut keys may be used.

Excel function names are in uppercase, eg ROUND, SUM.

We sometimes advise you to search the Help file contents for further detail. We provide a key phrase to type into the *Answer Wizard* or the *Ask a Question* box:

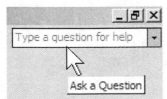

CATEGORY: 1 Design

This category comprises two skill sets:

> 1.1 Specification

> 1.2 Security

This section will give you the knowledge to answer these searching questions that your employer or auditor may ask:

- How do you know this spreadsheet is what is wanted?

- Has the design been reviewed and approved by the system owner?

- What change controls do you have in place?

- How often do you backup your key spreadsheets and data?

- How many previous versions can you go back to, on what dates?

- How often do you verify your backups, are they secure and off-site?

- What traceability is there on information exchanged between corporate data sources and spreadsheets for consolidation and reporting?

- Have you measured the sensitivity of your financial models to changes in input parameters?

Organisations in regulated environments may have to comply with standards relating to traceability, Standard Operating Procedures (SOP), validation testing and verification of calculation methods. Those responsible for enforcing SOPs need to explain to a spreadsheet creator how their work process and product is affected by these standards.

Skill set: 1.1 Specification

1.1.1   Define spreadsheet specifications.

A *Specification* is a statement of *how* the spreadsheet is to meet *the user requirements*. A specification can be as simple as explanatory text in a worksheet, or as complex as separate legal documentation. There is an example specification for a payroll spreadsheet on page 10.

The *purpose* of the spreadsheet is a statement of why it was created, the problem it solves, and the part it plays in the decisions and documentation of the business process.

The list of *user requirements* is the most important part of a specification. Clear requirements provide the basis for acceptance testing, and say what the user does and does not require, preventing disagreement as to when the work is complete.

Usability features are help text, navigation aids, protection, and automation of common tasks. Specify these so that the intended users can operate the spreadsheet correctly, avoid misunderstandings, and achieve their objectives easily.

The *author,* the initial creator of the spreadsheet, is often also the person responsible for maintaining it.

The *version history* describes the stages of evolution of the spreadsheet.

Such information may be recorded in:

1.   the spreadsheet File Properties;

2.   documentation worksheets;

3.   separate document files.

If the spreadsheet is to be sent to people who should not see internal, personal, or private information, remove this data from the released version of the spreadsheet. Do not rely on hiding it to maintain confidentiality. Section 5.1.3 on page 139 describes how cells, formulas, rows, columns, and sheets can be unhidden.

Use the spreadsheet file Properties

Use <u>F</u>ile > Proper<u>t</u>ies to fill in data that makes it easier to search for files, and to identify the author when questions arise. Typically these are: Title, Subject, Author, Category, Keywords, and Comments; and where appropriate the Manager and Company. The Custom properties allow you to add more detail. Keep contact details for those responsible for development, maintenance, and supplying data.

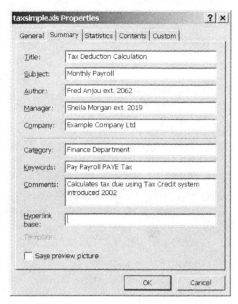

File properties initially contain the username (the registered user of the software) as the author.

Excel can prompt you to fill in the file properties each time you save. On the <u>T</u>ools menu, click <u>O</u>ptions, and on the <u>G</u>eneral tab check <u>P</u>rompt for workbook properties:

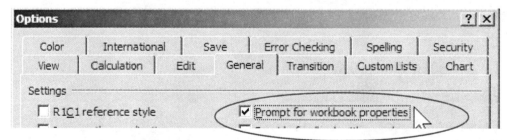

Place documentation in worksheets

Keep documentation close to where it used so that it can be updated along with what it refers to. Otherwise, neglected documentation or cell comments may become actually misleading. Section 1.1.2 on page 11 shows how to use cell comments to store information that may be needed by the user at the time of data entry.

Place in a separate *Instructions* worksheet the user instructions and explanatory notes on calculations and dependencies on external data sources. The example shown in the following screen shot is from the spreadsheet **TaxSimple.xls**, which is one of the sample workbooks accompanying this book.

22	Outputs			
23		*Periodic:*	After entering the gross pay, print off the sheet as a record for the employee.	
24				
25	Formulas	*Column*	*Heading*	*Calculation*
26		C	Cumulative Gross Pay to date	The first row is the same as the entry in col.B, subsequent rows accumulate the sum of the pay for the current period and the previous cumulative pay in col.C.

|◄ ◄ ► ►| \ TaxCalc / TestCases / Notes \ **Specification** / |◄ |

When to use separate document files

Use separate documentation in cases where the documentation is extensive. This may be appropriate for user training manuals or operating procedures such as how to enter data, check for errors and correct them.

Keep a note in the workbook of where that separate document is so that it is not forgotten about.

Interviews and project notes are usually kept in word processed documents. Create a separate document of technical design notes for the maintainer. These include:

- Internal or hidden data;
- External links to other files or corporate databases;
- Data populated by program code such as live data feeds;
- Any special setup instructions for first time use;
- Passwords to access protected areas;
- Test plans (who applies what tests to the spreadsheet when and how)
- Test records (the results of executing the test plans)

How much specification is enough?

Describe assumptions and limitations, even apparently obvious ones. They may not be obvious to the user or to the next person who maintains the spreadsheet; or to you at some time in the future. You may already have had the experience of trying to make sense of someone else's large and sprawling spreadsheet. State what is intentionally omitted from the scope of a spreadsheet project, as that is the hardest thing to check later.

Exactly how detailed a specification needs to be depends on the relationship between the person who creates the spreadsheet structure and the user. If you are creating a spreadsheet for yourself, you need to record whatever you think is not obvious from looking at it. What is obvious to you, while you are immersed in work, can be easily forgotten later, outside that context.

Designing a spreadsheet for others to use

The extent of user-friendly features that you need to design in will depend on:

- The number of people who will be using the spreadsheet

- The wider the diversity of their skill level

- The lower their skill level (consider skills certification)

- The greater the turnover of staff who use it

Test the spreadsheet with different user groups in order to reduce the likelihood that a confusing or awkward layout will induce users to create errors.

- Can & do the users access the online help in text cells, cell comments, and instruction worksheets?

- Can & do the users access written documentation or co-worker assistance?

- How adequately does the help provided resolve the questions of different user groups about using the spreadsheet?

- In the usability evaluation notes, do you find user problem comments like 'slow, time-consuming, awkward, tedious, intensive, unclear, not sure, confused, bewildering, hard to navigate / follow / find, repetitious, duplication'?

✎ 1.1.1 Check your knowledge (answers on page 165)

1. What are the risks in omitting a specification for creating a spreadsheet?
2. What are five key items to include in a specification and which is the most important?
3. What kind of information would you use *File Properties* for?

An example of a written specification

User requirement: calculate the tax due on employee salaries each month.

Examples of acceptance test cases are given on page 130.

The basis for calculation is as specified in the Irish Revenue Commissioners document 'PAYE Notice to Employers 2004' which states:

1) The standard rate of tax (20%) is applied to gross pay up to the standard rate cut-off point (SRCOP) for the pay period.
2) Any balance of gross pay over SRCOP is taxed at the higher rate (42%)
3) The gross tax is reduced by the tax credit to give the net tax payable.
4) The figures for tax credit and the SRCOP are defined in a Tax Deduction Card for each employee issued to the employer by the Revenue Commissioners. An example of this card is shown following:

Sample Tax Deduction Card for A.N. Employee

A	B	C	D	E	F	G	H	I
Date of payment	Gross Pay	Cumul Gross Pay to date	Cumul Std Rate Cut off Point	Cumul Tax due at Std rate	Cumul Tax due at Higher rate	Cumul Tax Credit	Cumul Tax (not less than zero)	Tax deducted this period
			1644.45			123.34		
			3288.89			246.68		
			4933.33			370.02		

The figures are calculated to full precision and displayed to 2 decimal places.

Calculation details (Source: http://www.revenue.ie/wnew/employ.pdf)
Col. A: Enter the date; Col. B Enter Gross Pay; Col. C is the cumulative of Col. B
Columns D and G are supplied by the Tax Office in the Tax Deduction Card.
Col. E: Enter the lower of column 3 or 4 multiplied by standard rate of tax
Col. F: Where Col. C minus Col. D is positive enter the result multiplied by the higher rate of tax. Where negative enter zero.
Col. H: is the sum of cols. E and F less Col. G
Col. I: Subtract the cumulative tax (H) for the last pay period from the cumulative tax (H) for this pay period and enter the result here.

> **1.1.2   Use cell comments and descriptions to list sources and assumptions.**

Cell comments are best used for information that does not need to be always visible but can be called up if required.

Descriptions, entered as text labels in the spreadsheet, are best used for instructions that must always be seen, or explanations for infrequently used parts of the spreadsheet.

Sources of input data are the names of documents providing input either by keyboard entry or by external file links and database queries.

Assumptions are data taken as known in a given context, limitations on scope and timeframe, and projected forecasts or expectations of the future.

User access levels are implemented by protected or hidden cells, rows, columns, or worksheets, where a password is needed to access certain parts of the spreadsheet. Users and maintainers need to be informed of what is available to them.

To add a comment to a cell:

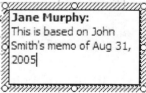

1. Click the cell you want to comment on.

2. On the Insert menu, click Comment, or press Shift+F2.

3. In the box, type the comment text.

4. If you don't want your name in the comment, select and delete the name.

5. When you finish typing the text, click outside the comment box.

Comments

The appearance of comment indicators or comments is controlled by <u>T</u>ools > <u>O</u>ptions > View tab, Comments:

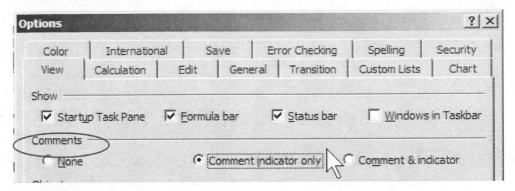

A comment indicator is a red triangle in the top right corner of a cell. Hold the mouse over the cell to see the text pop up, or select the cell and press Shift+F2 to edit it.

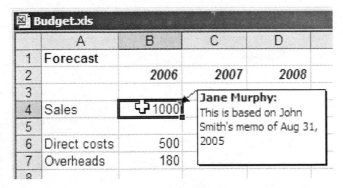

To print comments on the end of each page, use <u>F</u>ile > Page Set<u>u</u>p > Sheet tab, and in the Co<u>m</u>ments options select At end of sheet.

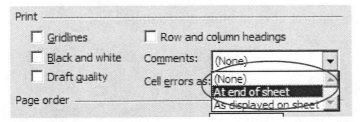

In addition, there is an option on that tab for Row and column headings which makes it easier to identify the coordinates of a cell in a printout.

Assumptions

Don't scatter assumptions throughout the spreadsheet. Bring them together into one area to make it easier to review and update them. This reduces the risk of someone using a spreadsheet while unaware that its assumptions do not apply in the present instance. Say what ranges of values apply to the assumptions, and what conditions would cause you to change your assumptions, such as a change in bank interest rates.

Section 2.1.2 on page 41 also recommends isolating control variables.

State the authoritative sources and the date on which assumptions were current and when they should be reviewed. You can add a reminder in a cell using the IF function, as shown below:

Example of a worksheet showing assumptions

| D2 | ▼ | fx =IF(C2<NOW(),"Review is needed","") |

Projections.xls

	A	B	C	D	E
1		Last reviewed on	01-Jan-04	by JM	
2		Next review due by	01-Jan-05	**Review is needed**	
3					
4		*Assumptions*	*Normal*	*Overtime*	
5		Hourly paid workers rate	10	15	
6		Monthly paid rate	2000	n/a	
7		Production tonnes/hr	123	112.5	
8		Sales units/month	10000		
9		Sales increase/month	0.05		
10		*Other assumptions (J. Doe Nov. 2005)*			
11		Overtime only applies 6pm to 11pm			
12		Price is not changed over the projected period			

1.1.2 Check your knowledge *(answers on page 165)*

1. What are the risks in omitting comments or supporting text?

2. When would you use text in cells rather than comments?

3. List three things you would use comments for.

> **1.1.3   Be explicit about conventions, methods, functions, formats, and policies.**

Calculation methods may also be called steps, rules, or algorithms.

Functions are the built-in spreadsheet functions such as SUM.

Formats can be used to achieve a consistent style. Below, we describe physical and logical layout, ordering and grouping data areas, spacing, and print setup.

Policies are organisational requirements for how spreadsheets are written or used.

Calculation methods

Ensure the owner of a spreadsheet knows what calculation methods are used. Users may need to be able to change starting figures or choose from alternative calculation methods. Complex calculation methods, processing sequences, and short-cut tricks, obvious when building the spreadsheet, will not be so obvious after a lapse of time. This picture shows a cell documenting a calculation method:

| F8 | | f_x | =C6+NPV($D$8,D6:H6) | | | | | |

NPV.xls

	A	B	C	D	E	F	G	H	I
1	Project NPV								
2									
3		Year	2005	2006	2007	2008	2009	2010	
4		Investment	1000	2000	0	0	0	0	
5		Income	0	500	1000	1000	1000	500	
6		Net Cash flow	-1000	-1500	1000	1000	1000	500	
7									
8		Net Present Value at		5%	=	557			
9		Note: we are using end of period discounting as per SOP ACC-2000-07-17							

Document the source of each of the equations, calculations, and algorithms that you have used. In a regulated environment like the pharmaceutical industry, the calculation methods and functions must be validated.

Functions

Some spreadsheet functions can work in different ways depending on a convention that you select with a function argument[3]. Explicitly include all the optional arguments when using functions, so that you consciously choose what they are to be, rather than assume that the default choice is correct. This also makes your choice clear to future users. For example, the YEARFRAC function calculates the fraction of the year represented by the number of whole days between two dates (the start_date and the end_date). It has a third optional argument basis, which defaults to *US (NASD) 30/360*. You should specify a basis:

```
YEARFRAC(start_date,end_date,basis)
```

Physical and Logical layout

Tidy up your spreadsheet and check its spelling. This has more than cosmetic value; it makes it more acceptable and credible. To avoid misunderstanding, ensure that the meaning of the text labels beside numbers is correct.

Remove any empty worksheets before distribution.

Give worksheets meaningful names rather than the default **Sheet1**, etc. To do this, either double-click the sheet tab and enter the name, or right-click the tab and choose **Rename** from the popup menu. Do not use spaces in sheet names, as this may cause trouble later if you use VBA or Data Access code to refer to sheets.

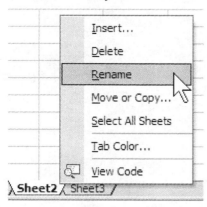

---

[3] Argument: one of the items that appears inside the brackets of a function. For example, in =MIN(C4,15) C4 and 15 are the two arguments.

Lay out the spreadsheet to make it easy to understand and use, to reflect the natural data flow from input through calculation into output. Make the data flow of the spreadsheet follow the same arrangement as the source paper documents with which the user is already familiar.

Where you have data that is infrequently updated, use sheet protection to prevent it from being accidentally overtyped by users unfamiliar with its meaning. Even a blank password would at least make changing the data a conscious act. Separate such data from regularly entered data, or protect the cells so that updating them has to be a conscious choice. Excel 2002 and later has the ability to provide separate passwords for different areas of a worksheet.

Ordering and grouping data into areas

Arrange the spreadsheet so that it can be read in the conventional expected order (in the Western world, anyway) of top down and left to right. Observe how much is visible at one time in the window. If the user has to scroll around too much, they may miss important elements of the spreadsheet. A well constructed spreadsheet saves the user from wasting time looking for data. It can also prevent wrong decisions where important information was not seen because it was in an unexpected place.

Use View > Zoom to get an overview of a sheet. When viewed with Zoom factors less than 40%, Excel also shows the names assigned to each range:

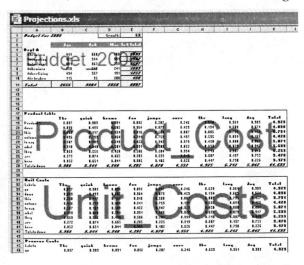
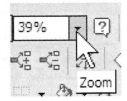

In the previous illustration, the Zoom dropdown box has a yellow *screen tip* displayed beside it. To enable this for all MS Office applications, on the <u>T</u>ools menu click <u>C</u>ustomize; on the Options tab check Show Screen<u>T</u>ips on toolbars:

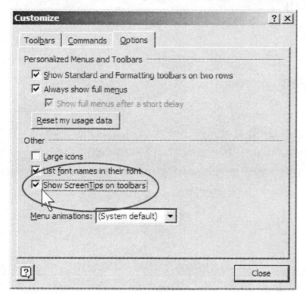

A special input area, or an area that collects and presents inputs in one table, makes it easy to print a record for the auditors of the input data. Ensure that the print areas correspond to all that should be printed.

Lay out the spreadsheet so that it can be expanded easily. Separate the blocks of data so that insertion into, or deletion from, one block does not damage others.

Gaps between logical areas, rows formatted with extra height, and columns formatted with extra width, also help readability by providing white space to guide the eye.

Isolate blocks of similar formulas for safe and convenient copying. This can be done by placing gaps between blocks of copied formulas. Then, if the user selects the current region to move or copy in that range and no less, the integrity of the formulas is maintained and unintended cells are not accidentally copied or moved.

Learn how to use the shortcut keys described on page 161 to select and navigate around the edges of a data region. A *data region* is a range that contains data and is bounded by empty cells or worksheet borders.

Use consistent workbook structures. For example:

- Save commonly used workbooks as templates

- Use styles, fonts and colour with consistent meanings. (See below for an example of defining format styles)

- Always list products in the same order

- Adopt conventions for naming directories, files, worksheets and ranges.

A basic usability rule is: *avoid surprises*. Users can become familiar with a spreadsheet faster if they follow a house style, then time is not lost learning the structure of every different spreadsheet from scratch. There is still the risk that people can become used to one particular order of entry or file location. They may then incorrectly assume that it applies in a spreadsheet where the designer has not followed the expected order.

Cell formats and styles

Use font effects, such as size, bold, italic, colour, borders and shading, in moderation. John Raffensperger's[4] rule is: 'Format for description, not decoration'. Format or shade the cells to make their use distinctive, for example by applying a light blue shading to input cells. Be aware that red and green are not clearly distinguishable in some forms of visual impairment.

Avoid merging cells as they can cause problems with copy and paste operations. Also, when merging, Excel places only the upper-leftmost data in the selected range into the resulting merged cell. If there is data in other cells, the data is deleted. Consider instead using the cell format *Center across selection*:

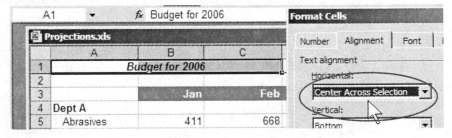

---

[4] www.mang.canterbury.ac.nz/people/jfraffen/sscom/index.htm Spreadsheet style

To define a style that can be applied easily to any cell, on the **Format** menu, click **Style**; and type the name of the new style, eg, *InputCell*:

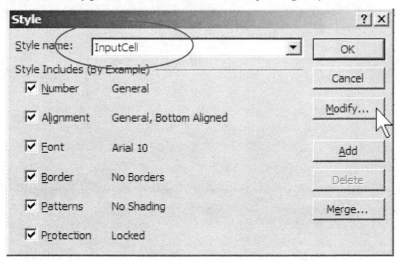

Click **Modify**, click the **Patterns** tab, and click the light blue shading:

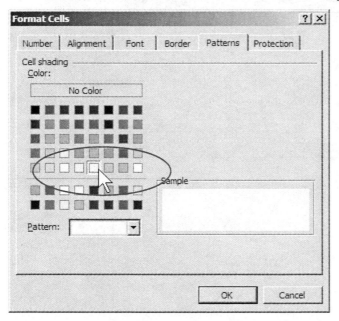

Click the OK button on the **Format Cell** dialog. Click Add on the **Style** dialog. Click the Cancel button to close the dialog. If you click OK, it will also apply the new style to the currently selected cell.

Apply that style to input cells by using **Format** > **Style** and selecting *InputCell*. If you decide to change the style for input cells, for example to make the font Courier or to put a border around each cell, you only have to modify this named style and all cells with that style show the modified format.

When spreadsheets are to be exchanged internationally, be aware that local formats for money and dates can cause confusion. Use month names, eg 12-Jul-2006, rather than the ambiguous 12/07/06.

Right-justify row descriptive labels to draw attention to the row of data that follows. Indent subheadings under main headings. Use bold font and centred or right-justified headings for columns of numbers. Do not left align numeric cells as that would make them look like text entries. This screenshot shows some of these ideas:

	A	B	C	D	E
	Projections.xls				
1	*Budget for 2006*	*€'000*		*Growth:*	*5%*
2					
3		**Jan**	**Feb**	**Mar**	**Qtr1 total**
4	**Dept A**				
5	Abrasives	411	668	760	*1839*
6	Accounting	427	544	331	*1302*
7	Actuators	381	967	239	*1587*
8	Adhesives	828	540	241	*1609*
9	Advertising	494	567	191	*1252*
10	Air brakes	115	95	288	*498*
11	*Total*	*2656*	*3381*	*2050*	*8087*

Policies

Understand the reasons for any policies adopted by your organisation regarding security, access, prescribed calculation methods, validation methods, and so on. This prevents effort wasted in writing calculation methods that have to be rewritten because they breach organisational IT policy and standards.

Example of an End User Computing Policy

XYZ Bank Ltd End User Computing Policy Section 4-Spreadsheets

Document: EUC-POLICY-4 Version: 2.12. Date: 5 April 2005

Location: `\\server\corporate\policies\it\euc\spreadsheet_dev.doc`

1) Every spreadsheet must be reviewed by the supervisor and submitted for risk assessment.

2) Mission-critical spreadsheets will follow the standard IT development process of having more than one person on the team. The process will include a specification phase, project documentation, a change board, weekly progress reports, final acceptance testing by users, and review by internal audit.

3) Important spreadsheets will have weekly progress reports, acceptance testing by users, and sign-off by the supervisor.

4) Non-critical spreadsheets shall be signed-off by the supervisor before being accepted into use.

Example of a Spreadsheet Style policy

XYZ Bank Ltd Policies on spreadsheet style

Policy: EUC-POLICY-5 Version: 1.09. Date: 1 June 2005

Location: `\\server\corporate\policies\it\euc\spreadsheet_style.doc`

1) Other than simple totals, every spreadsheet calculation method, financial function (NPV,IRR,...) and add-in (such as for real-time data interchange) **must** be accompanied by a note that refers back to the documented Standard Operating Procedure for performing this calculation and provides the date, name and contact point of the person who signed off that it conforms to company standards.

2) The built-in Excel functions for NPV assume that the investment begins one period before the date of the value1 cash flow and ends with the last cash flow in the list. The NPV calculation is based on future cash flows. If your first cash flow occurs at the beginning of the first period, the first value must be added to the NPV result, not included in the values arguments. If the cash flows are not periodic, use XNPV with a date range.

3) Our house style is:

a) Every worksheet is protected;

b) Regular data input cells are unprotected and have a light beige background and a solid border;

c) Protected input cells for infrequent changes have a yellow background;

d) Headings are bold, right justified over numeric data;

e) Red font or background is reserved for error messages.

4) Our policy on spreadsheet development is defined in document EUC-POLICY-4.

1.1.3 Check your knowledge (*answers on page 166*)

1. What are the risks in not documenting how functions are used?

2. List three important points about spreadsheet style.

3. Does your organisation have policies on spreadsheet development?

Skill set: 1.2 Security

1.2.1	Make regular secure backups of spreadsheet and related files.

A *backup* is a copy of a known correct file kept in a secure place so that you can restore it to recover from data loss or corruption.

Make a backup immediately before making a change that you may want to undo. You can revert to the previously known good state if you decide to abandon the changes you just made. Experienced spreadsheet builders save often.

Copy the spreadsheet files to a secure medium independent of your local PC – eg a diskette, CDROM, or tape, kept offsite in a fireproof safe. If your network administrator automatically backs up data stored on the server every night, you can copy your files to that server drive so that it is included in the backup.

Verify whether the backup medium is readable, complete, and corresponds to the original. You can do this by restoring a file from backup, as a test. If you use tape, always use the option to verify after writing the tape.

Another method is to **File > Save As** with a new filename as soon as you open the file to avoid accidentally over-writing the original file.

When starting a new spreadsheet, always **Save As** a different file name than the default **Book1**. It is too easy for you or another user to later save another **Book1** over that file.

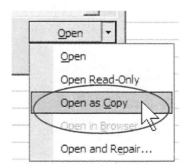

You can also open Excel spreadsheets using the **File > Open as Copy** command. You see the option when you click the drop down arrow beside the **Open** button in the Open Dialog. Then when you save, Excel is saving to a copy file.

Excel has an **Autosave** option which saves a worksheet automatically at set intervals. Therefore if you recover an autosaved spreadsheet, you do not know what precise state it was in at the instant of saving, and so must spend time checking it. It is safest to recover to a version that you know you saved in a correct state. To enable Autosave: on the **Tools** menu, click **Options**, and then click the **Save** tab. Select **the Save AutoRecover info every** check box. In the **minutes** box, specify how often you want Excel to save files.

Protect your important programs and files from viruses and Trojans from files downloaded from the Internet, or received by email. To reduce the risk of macro infection in Excel files, set Tools > Macros > Security level to High or Medium. Also ensure that the PC has a resident virus scanner that is updated every day.

1.2.1 Check your knowledge (*answers on page 166*)

What are the risks in omitting to make backups?

CATEGORY: 1 Design, Skill set: 1.2 Security

> **1.2.2   Maintain separately saved versions of spreadsheets in development.**

A *version* refers to a known state in the development of a spreadsheet.

A *release* is a version that has been released to users.

When you want to update the formulas or structure in a spreadsheet, create a new version. Then the previous method of working can always be referred to as a comparison. Keep the new version in a separate development directory until you have finished validating it, so that it is not accidentally used by mistake.

An independent review of changes to any work product is the one most beneficial process improvement that organisations can make. You can use workbook comparison tools (on page 163) to verify that the differences between the before and after versions are only what they should be.

Keep a *version history* worksheet page as a log of changes, showing who made them, when, and their reasons – eg, enhancement requests, bug fixes. A user can check the status of this worksheet to assure themselves that that they are using the correct version of the spreadsheet.

A *release* must be retained so that corresponding linked or source data files can be read with the appropriate version of the spreadsheet.

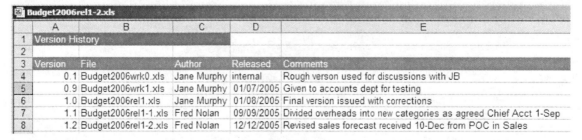

	A	B	C	D	E
1	Version History				
2					
3	Version	File	Author	Released	Comments
4	0.1	Budget2006wrk0.xls	Jane Murphy	internal	Rough verson used for discussions with JB
5	0.9	Budget2006wrk1.xls	Jane Murphy	01/07/2005	Given to accounts dept for testing
6	1.0	Budget2006rel1.xls	Jane Murphy	01/08/2005	Final version issued with corrections
7	1.1	Budget2006rel1-1.xls	Fred Nolan	09/09/2005	Divided overheads into new categories as agreed Chief Acct 1-Sep
8	1.2	Budget2006rel1-2.xls	Fred Nolan	12/12/2005	Revised sales forecast received 10-Dec from POC in Sales

An authorised list of users helps to ensure that updates are distributed to all who use it (and nobody else). That way, everybody is using the same version. When multiple versions are in use, more demands are placed on support staff to keep track of which operations are appropriate to which version of spreadsheet or add-in.

Clearly label the current release and date to avoid the risk of a user entering into an out-of-date release of the spreadsheet. This should also appear in page header or footer sections on printouts, so readers know which release was used to create it. To set up a header or footer, on the <u>V</u>iew menu click <u>H</u>eader and Footer:

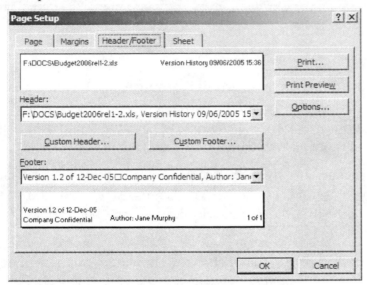

The printout shows these at the top and bottom of the page:

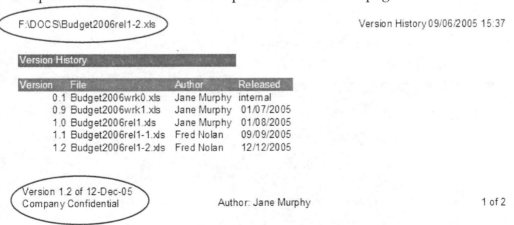

1.2.2 Check your knowledge (*answers on page 167*)

What are the risks of poor version control and unmanaged changes?

1.2.3   Understand the security limitations of password protection.

A *password* is applied as an extra protection to worksheet and workbook protection. It makes it harder for an unauthorised user to remove the protection. But there are limitations to the security offered by passwords.

Worksheet password protection is weak and can be defeated by software you can find on the Internet, as this screen shot of a status bar shows:

Sheet1 Password Broken in 15128 attempts

Workbook file protection is more robust but can still be defeated if you chose short or common words as passwords.

To protect formulas from accidental changes, remove cell protection from the input cells then protect the sheet with a password. Cell protection is on by default. If you have only a few formulas to protect, select the whole sheet, unprotect all cells, then go back and protect the few. On the Tools menu, click Protection, and click Protect Sheet. Enter the password and click OK:

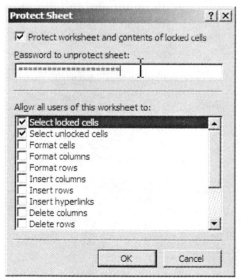

Maintain a list of spreadsheet passwords under secure access control. If you forget the password to a workbook, you lose access to what must be (because it is password protected!) important data. You could try a software tool that breaks passwords, but:

a)   It may take days or months to get past well-chosen passwords.

b)   The use of such tools may be restricted to security specialists under the immediate observation of the IT manager and Chief Security Officer.

c)   The purchase of such tools may be forbidden by company policy.

Workbook passwords

At the time you save a spreadsheet, you can specify a password that will be needed to open it again. Click Save As on the File menu, click General Options on the Tools menu:

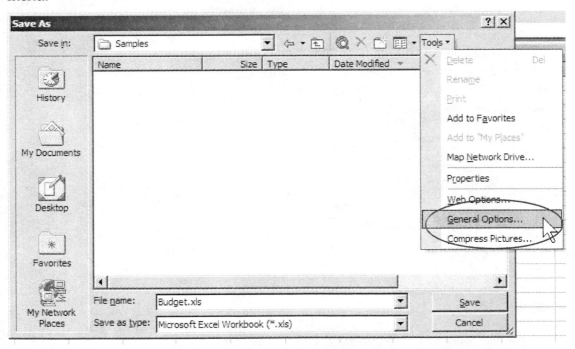

You then specify the password in this dialog:

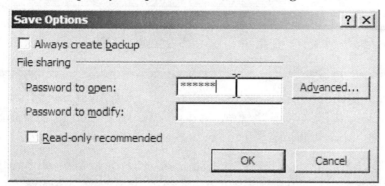

The **Advanced** button allows you to specify encryption schemes such as RC4 that are stronger than the default *Microsoft Office 97/2000 compatible*. Even then, a hacker can break encryption given two or more versions of the file, eg, a backup and an edited copy.

1.2.3 Check your knowledge (*answers on page 167*)

1. What are the limitations of worksheet password security?

2. What are the limitations of workbook password security?

> **1.2.4   Use passwords of at least 8 mixed case, non-alphanumeric characters.**

The longer a password is, and the more mixed its contents, the less likelihood there is of it being guessed or bypassed by a tool. Automated password breaking programs work by trying many combinations of letters, or lists of common words like *admin*.

Passwords should have 8 characters or more, with mixed case and non-alphabetic characters. Most people don't try very hard and use *secret*, or other common passwords. These are easily guessed by hackers who use software that tries lists of common words.

A way to create a memorable password

Think of a line from a favourite song or story, preferably not the first or most famous catchphrase line. Use the first, second, or last letters of each word, mix the case, and you can get a longish password.

Another idea is to change some letters to numbers or vice versa. For example, AFAICR becomes @F@1cr. Some popular substitutions are:

Original	Change to		Original	Change to
letter A	symbol @		letter S	digit 5
letter I	digit 1		letter T	symbol +
letter B	digit 8		letter Z	number 2
letter O	digit 0		digit 1	symbol !

Passwords should:

- be long and mysterious
- protect the owner
- be used by one person, not a group
- be changed periodically
- not be left out for everyone to see.

1.2.4 Check your knowledge (*answers on page 167*)

Which of these are good passwords and which are not good?

      a.   0DbtPtP@c

      b.   secret

      c.   aB6%KK0-$3

      d.   administrator

      e.   1!2"3£4$

      f.   guess

      g.   rTrNrHaVsN

      h.   password

CATEGORY: 2 Input

This comprises one skill set: 2.1 Set-up

We recommend:

- Formulas should not be too complex to understand

- Clean up spreadsheets to reduce the risk of errors

- Range names help reduce misplaced references

- Don't have multiple instances of a number that is used as an assumption or parameter

- Be explicit about the units of measure and check conversions

- Be careful about settings that affect data precision

- Know what to do when the recalculation setting is set to manual

Skill set: 2.1 Set-up

2.1.1	Simplify long formulas and use named ranges.

Simplify a formula that is too complex to understand at first glance. A formula with only a long list of cell references (=A14+B17+C20+D35+E41...) may be tedious but not too complex to understand. By *complex* we mean overlong, hard to understand, easily misread and so liable to people introducing defects when they modify them.

Long complex formulas could be described humorously as *write-only*; nobody else can read them. If you have to puzzle out a formula, it's too big. Therefore, break it up into intermediate formulas in the way you do when you are trying to understand it. This is done by adding more rows or columns to show the intermediate steps. For example, instead of repeating the INDEX function in this formula:

`=IF(ISNA(A9),"",IF(INDEX(Table,A9,5)=0,"",INDEX(Table,A9,5)))`

Place `=INDEX(Table,A9,5)` in its own cell, say B9, and then use this formula:

`=IF(ISNA(A9),"",IF(B9=0,"",B9))`

If the user does not need to see the intermediate cells, hide them. However, this advice of adding intermediate rows and columns is difficult to follow for block copies where the formula is copied across *and* down. The chain of calculation logic is harder to follow if blocks of intermediate steps are placed on other parts of the worksheet or on different worksheets.

Nested functions result in many brackets (parentheses) in a formula. You may find it difficult to match up the opening and closing bracket of each function and that slows you down in working out what the formula does. Excel 2000 and later colour-codes the brackets, as you enter them, and briefly flashes the pair when you enter a closing bracket.

To step through the calculations in a complex formula

Excel 2002 and later has a menu item <u>T</u>ools > Formula A<u>u</u>diting > Evaluate <u>F</u>ormula, which can help in tracing the calculation steps.

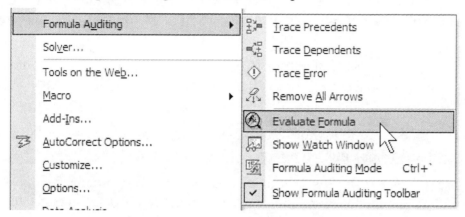

In this example, we have so far evaluated the first two references in F8 and the values are shown in the dialog box. The next click of the **Evaluate** button would calculate the NPV function:

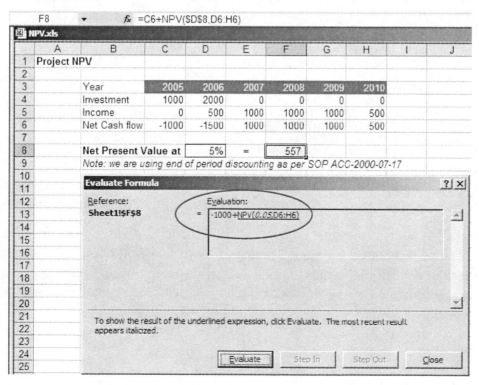

Range Names

A range is an area of one or more cells, usually contiguous but not necessarily so. A range name is a user-defined name that you create as a convenient mnemonic for the address of a range of cells. For example, you may give the address A1:Z100 the range name **Database**.

- Range names improve reliability. If you need to change references to the range, you only have to change the definition of the range name. Then every formula that uses it will refer to the new address.

- They are a good way to identify control factors. A name like TAXRATE is more readable than an absolute cell reference like Sheet2!$F$12.

- They are a safe way to link workbooks because the range name reference is maintained with the location. This is dealt with in section 3.3.8 on page 89.

- Range names must begin with a letter or underscore and contain only letters or digits, no spaces or other special characters. They cannot look like addresses such as A1. To avoid a clash with the R1C1 reference style (shown on page 143), they cannot be simply R, C, RC, or start with C1 to C256 or R1 to R65536.

To create a workbook range name

Select the cell, range, or nonadjacent selections that you want to name. Then, either:

1. Click the Name box at the left end of the formula bar.
   Enter the name for the cells. If the name is already defined, Excel selects the range; it will not change the definition.

2. Or on the Insert menu, point to Name, and then click Define. The Define Name dialog box is illustrated on page 37. In the Names in workbook box, enter the name for the cells. If the name is already defined, its definition is changed.

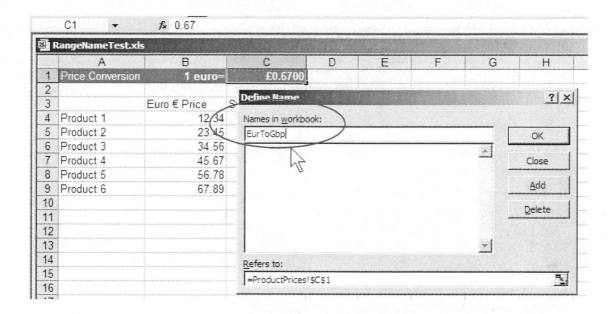

Exercise: create and apply a range name

In this exercise you will create a range name and apply it to existing formulas.

Open the file **RangeNameTest.xls**[5]. Note that the formulas in cells C4:C9 all have an absolute reference to $C$1. That cell contains a conversion rate from EUR (euro) to GBP (British pound).

We shall change the reference to C1 to a range name *EURtoGBP*. Select cell C1 on the sheet *ProductPrices*. Click in the name box in the formula bar, and enter *EURtoGBP*.

---

[5] Download the example workbooks from http://www.sysmod.com/sbp

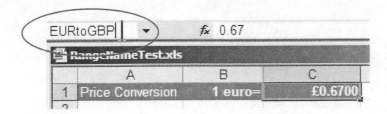

Select cell C4 again, and note that Excel did not automatically change the reference for us. Rather than retyping formulas, we can apply the range name to all the formulas in one step. On the Insert menu, point to Name, and then click Apply. (There is only one name defined, so it is already selected. If we had more than one name, you could select one or more.) The next picture shows this dialog box. Click OK.

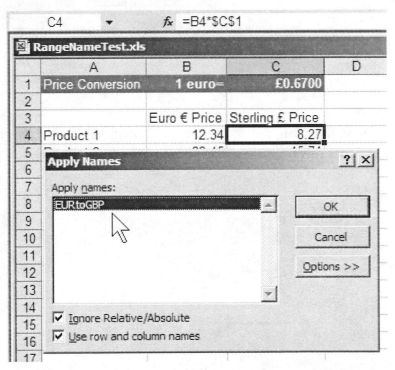

Leave the two checkboxes selected. *Ignore Relative/Absolute* replaces references with names regardless of the type of reference. *Use row and column names* inserts *implied intersection* names where the row or column reference is included in an existing range name. See the note on page 68 for a definition of *intersections*.

Now examine cells C4 to C9 and Excel has applied the name to the formulas. This screen shot is shown in Formula View to display all the formulas:

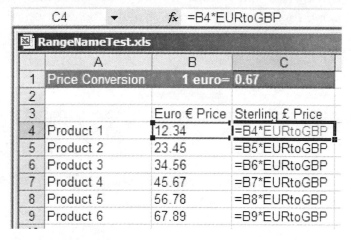

To examine defined names

On the <u>I</u>nsert menu, point to <u>N</u>ame, and then click <u>D</u>efine. The *Define Name* dialog box shows the global names and any local names (described on page 40) for the current sheet. Before deleting range names that appear to be unused in the workbook, be sure they are not referred to by linked workbooks or VBA code.

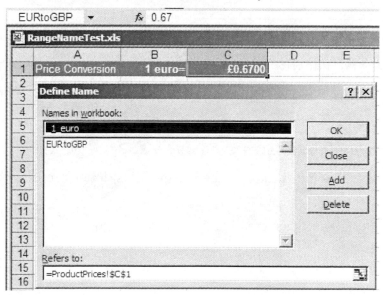

To create a list of defined names

Locate on the worksheet an area with two empty columns. The list will contain two columns: one for the name; and one for a description of the name. Select a cell that will be the upper-left corner of the list. On the Insert menu, point to Name, and then click Paste. In the Paste Name dialog box, click Paste List. In this picture, we pasted the list beginning in cell E2:

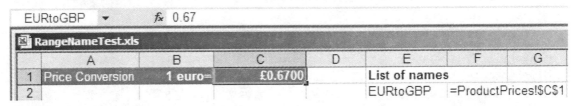

	A	B	C	D	E	F	G
1	Price Conversion	1 euro=	£0.6700		List of names		
2					EURtoGBP	=ProductPrices!$C$1	

Advanced use of range names

There are ways to create and use range names that are not documented in the Excel Help. If you want to know about local/global names, names for formulas or dynamic ranges, you can learn more from these web sites:

http://www.robbo.com.au Navigator Utilities. Mark Robinson's free add-in helps you to navigate through Sheets, Links, and Named Ranges, even hidden ones.

http://www.cpearson.com/excel/named.htm

Working With Named Ranges In Excel by Chip Pearson, Microsoft MVP.

http://www.excelsig.org/PastMtgs/0110/Creating_Range_Names.htm

How many ways can you define a Range Name?

2.1.1 Check your knowledge (*answers on page 168*)

1. What are the advantages and disadvantages of breaking long formulas into short ones?

2. Why are range names better when creating links between workbooks?

2.1.2	Isolate constants into their own cells.

To *isolate* means to remove a numeric constant from a formula and place it in a cell of its own.

Isolate constants, rather than embedding (*hard coding*) literal numbers in formulas. A figure, assumed to be constant at the time the spreadsheet was created, may turn out in time to need revision, and therefore it is really a variable. An example is a tax rate or a conversion factor. The benefit of putting a constant into its own cell is that if its value ever does change, it need only be changed in one place. If it was a constant repeated in several formulas, some instances may not be changed, which leads to inconsistent calculations and incorrect results. You don't need to do this to numbers that really are constant like 1 or 100 used in percentage calculations.

Change this: to this:

	B3	▼	f_x =B2*21%

NamedConstant.xls

	A	B
1		
2	Sales	100
3	Tax	=B2*21%
4	Total	=B2+B3

	TaxRate	▼	f_x 21%

NamedConstant.xls

	A	B
1	Tax percent	0.21
2	Sales	100
3	Tax	=B2*TaxRate
4	Total	=B2+B3

Collect control variables together

An important kind of assumption is a *control variable*, also known as a *decision variable* or *model parameter*. Placing these together makes it easier to print out an assumptions page when running what-if scenarios, such as the best, worst and most likely cases. This page can be included in reports to provide a meaningful record of the assumptions that underlie the spreadsheet. Section 2.1.1 has recommendations on assigning range names to these for ease of reference.

Create range names for control variables

Give each of these key input cells a *range name* (described on page 36), to make the formulas that use them easier to understand. In entering a formula that refers to a control variable, it is difficult to point-and-click when the cell referred to is far distant or on a different sheet. It is less error prone to type a known range name or pick it from the list of range names obtained by pressing F3 (*Paste Name*). In the example below, in cell B3 we typed =B2* and pressed function key F3. To enter the name, we can simply click on *TaxRate* and click OK:

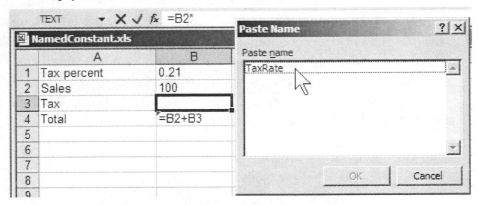

Watch for variations of the same number

When changing constants to cell or range references, be careful not to overlook instances of the number expressed slightly differently, eg an amount in C3 with 17.5% tax added might be found in several worksheets as:

```
=C3 + C3 * 17.5%
=C3 * ( 1 + 17.5/100 )
=C3 * 117.5%
=C3 * 1.175
=C3 * 47/40
```

Put the 17.5% into its own cell, eg G1, and then re-enter those formulas like this:

```
=C3*(1+$G$1)
```

Better still, apply the name TAXRATE to the range $G$1, then use:

```
=C3*(1+TAXRATE)
```

2.1.2 Check your knowledge (*answers on page 168*)

What is the risk in not isolating constants?

2.1.3   Identify units of measure and conversion calculations.

Examples of *units of measure* are metres or yards, kilos or pounds, days or months, or currency units. Make units of measure explicit, such as, the choice between metric or imperial measures. Otherwise a user may incorrectly enter data in the wrong units (eg pounds rather than kilogrammes) or scale (eg percents as parts per hundred or a fraction), and you end up 'adding apples and oranges'. In the following screen shot, how would you know whether this total is correct, or what it means?

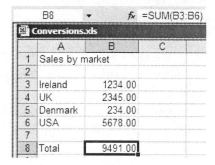

In spreadsheets that are to be used in more than one country, check for potential language, currency units, date formats, and other localisation problems, and forestall them by being explicit.

Isolate conversion factors into constant cells, as described on page 41.

---

http://www.hansard.act.gov.au/hansard/1998/pdfs/19981124.pdf ACT Hansard, 1998

'My office did prepare a table [that] double-counted dividends provided and projected... It was the most obvious and fundamental of mistakes in a simple spreadsheet. ... I do have one very contrite staffer who has otherwise been performing exemplary work.'

[Another speaker] 'What it shows is absolutely no financial credibility, no capacity, even when it is so obvious, to work out what the problem was. But even worse, [he] added the cash dividends out of the cash flow statement to profits from the operating statement. It is like adding apples and oranges.'

2.1.3 Check your knowledge (*answers on page 168*)

What is the risk in not identifying units of measurement?

2.1.4	Understand the "precision as displayed" setting.

Precision refers to the total number of significant digits to which numbers are stored, whether these digits are before or after the decimal place. Applying the **Precision as displayed** setting can lose precision in existing data.

Be aware that this setting truncates data. It can be used to fix the decimal places in data entry. It is in the **Tools** > **Options** > **Calculation** tab, under Workbook options.

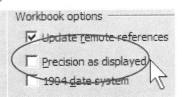

It is a workbook setting, so when you truncate (cut down) data to only what the display format shows, you lose the decimal places not shown. This also means that when you enter data, it ignores any figures you type beyond that. On the other hand, if you use **Edit** > **Copy** (Ctrl+C) to copy data and **Edit** > **Paste** (Ctrl+V) to paste it into a cell, this copies formats as well as values. So even if the target cell was formatted with a lower precision, the result is that the formatting of the pasted values takes effect first, then the data entry, so the precision is pasted along with the format.

A user may intend to enter data with a larger precision than displayed but they may not notice that decimal places have been truncated.

While this option is in effect, using the *Decrease Decimal* button on the Formatting toolbar will truncate data after the last decimal place displayed.

---

http://panko.cba.hawaii.edu/ssr/Cases.htm

Business Week 'How Personal Computers Can Trip Up Executives,' (2861) September 24, 1984, pp. 94-102, cited by Ray Panko, illustrates the problem of using *Precision as displayed* in Excel: Two 15,000-cell spreadsheets were used for a market projection. Numbers were rounded off to whole dollars, but an error during inputting caused the inflation multiplier of 1.06 to also be rounded off, becoming 1. Without inflation the market was underestimated by $36million, having serious consequences for the business.

Exercise in setting *Precision as displayed*

Start a new spreadsheet and type in the value 12.34567 into cells B3 to B8, and a SUM in B9. This is how it should look:

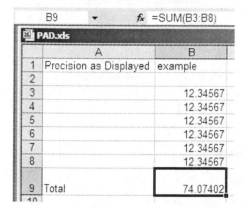

Now apply a numeric format with a different number of decimal places to each cell. Apply 4 decimal places in B4, 3 in B5 and so on down to no decimal places in B8.

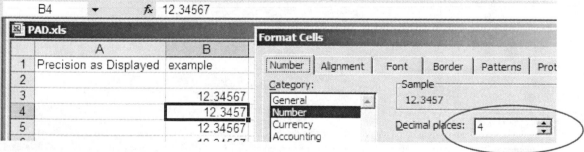

This is how it should look when done:

	B8	▼	f_x 12.34567

PAD.xls

	A	B
1	Precision as Displayed	example
2		
3		12.34567
4		12.3457
5		12.346
6		12.35
7		12.3
8		12
9	Total	74.07402

Select <u>T</u>ools > <u>O</u>ptions > Calculation tab, check <u>P</u>recision as displayed.

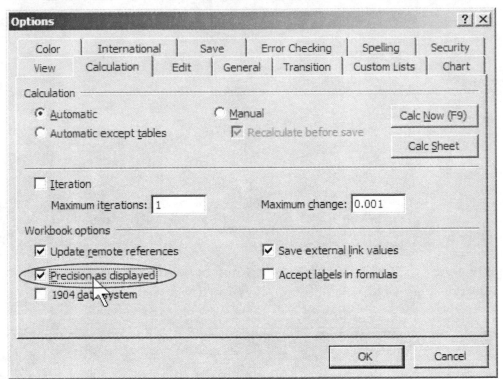

Click OK; Excel warns **Data will permanently lose accuracy**, click OK. In the following screen shot note that the data in B8 is now just 12, and the total has changed:

Show the formulas (Ctrl+`) and see that data has been lost in all the formatted cells:

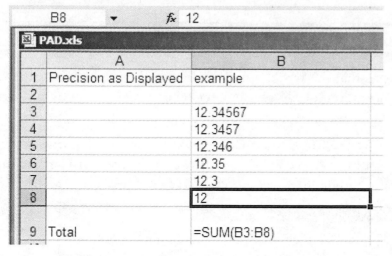

For further practice, select cell B3 and try the *Decrease Decimal* and *Increase Decimal* toolbar buttons.

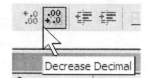

2.1.4 Check your knowledge (*answers on page 168*)

What is the risk in applying the Precision as displayed workbook setting?

> ### 2.1.5   Understand and use manual, automatic calculation.

Automatic calculation means that the workbook is recalculated every time an entry is changed. With *Manual* calculation it only recalculates when you tell it to by pressing the F9 key.

In Excel, the setting in the <u>T</u>ools > <u>O</u>ptions > Calculation tab is an *application* setting rather than a workbook setting (as it is in OpenOffice). Once you turn on manual calculation, it applies to all subsequent work in Excel until you turn it off again.

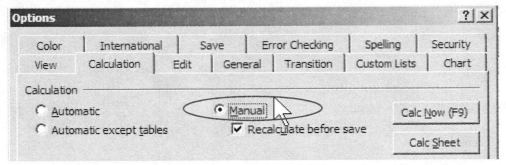

You usually apply this setting when working with large workbooks, for example those of a megabyte or more in size. Automatic recalculation slows input down. With manual calculation you wait until data entry is complete before pressing the F9 key to recalculate. But if you forget to press F9, you may print the results of incomplete calculations. Although Excel provides an option to recalculate when saving, it does not do that before printing.

You can force a recalculation by pressing Ctrl+Alt+F9. A search-and-replace of '=' with '=' will also force recalculation which may be required after a Copy and Paste.

You can recognise when a recalculation is necessary because Excel will show the word "Calculate" in the status bar at the bottom left of the window:

2.1.5 Check your knowledge (*answers on page 169*)

What is the risk of setting the calculation method to manual?

CATEGORY: 3 Calculation

This comprises three skill sets:

3.1 Fundamentals

This section deals with the fundamentals of calculation, the order of precedence of operators, which are misunderstood surprisingly often. We explain how to remove circular references. We describe array formulas and why you may use them.

3.2 Error Identification

This introduces one of the core skills of spreadsheet checking – how to look for incomplete inputs by tracing the chain of calculation. We describe the use of functions such as ISERROR to suppress error displays.

3.3 Error Correction

Now that you have found the errors, you need to know what caused them so you can fix them. We describe:

- incorrect absolute, relative, and external references;
- the wrong way to use Autosum;
- a comprehensive treatment of the obvious error values that begin with #, like #VALUE;
- more subtle errors which can be detected by finding inconsistencies in patterns of formulas;
- errors from structural changes which can be harder to find once made;
- how to build in cross-total or balancing checks;
- the right way to use Lookup functions

Skill set: 3.1 Fundamentals

3.1.1   Understand the order of precedence of mathematical operators.

The *order of precedence* is the order in which mathematical operations are carried out. Unlike a calculator that performs calculations in the order in which they are entered, Excel performs higher precedence operations before lower ones.

In an article in the Journal of Education for Business (Heldref Publications) dated Nov 1,2002, Ava Honan wrote 'Many university students enrolled in quantitative methods and basic computer programming courses do not understand the proper order of precedence that should be applied to mathematical operations.'

Excel <u>Help</u> gives this order of precedence for mathematical operators:

'If you combine several operators in a single formula, Excel performs the operations in the order shown in the following table. If a formula contains operators with the same precedence — for example, if a formula contains both a multiplication and division operator — Excel evaluates the operators from left to right.'

Operator	Description
: (colon) (single space) , (comma)	Reference operators
–	Negation (as in –1)
%	Percent
^	Exponentiation
* and /	Multiplication and division
+ and –	Addition and subtraction
&	Connects two strings of text (concatenation)
= < > <= >= <>	Comparison

To change the order of evaluation, enclose in parentheses the part of the formula to be calculated first. For example, the following formula produces 11 because multiplication has a higher priority than addition. The formula multiplies 2 by 3 and then adds 5 to the result.

```
=5+2*3
```

In contrast, if you use parentheses to change the syntax, the program adds 5 and 2 together and then multiplies the result by 3 to produce 21.

```
=(5+2)*3
```

Risk in misplacing parentheses

http://www.solutionmatrix.com/newsletter41.html
Cost/Benefit Newsletter June 2004 'We just lost our negotiating room - the pitfalls of Excel.'

'I found at the last minute that some very long spreadsheet formulas had parentheses out of place. When I put them where they belonged, our projected gains fell from $200M to $25M'. The writer gives two Excel formulas for estimating salary and overhead costs in Year 2 of a multi-year analysis. See if you can spot the error.

3.1.1 Check your knowledge (*answers on page 169*)

1. What is the result of −14+10*7 ?

2. What is the result of (−14+10)*7 ?

3.1.2   Remove circular references.

A *circular reference* happens when a formula refers directly or indirectly to its own cell address.

Circular references frequently are caused by mistake. They can be created intentionally as a means of iterating towards a solution, for example, in calculating interest on a balance that itself includes interest paid. Doing this requires enabling *Iteration* in the <u>T</u>ools > <u>O</u>ptions > Calculation tab:

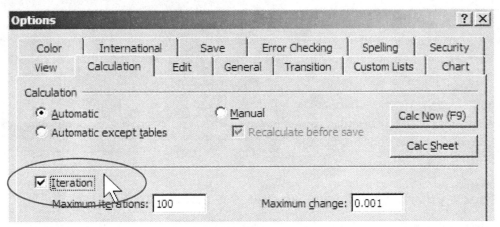

Iteration recalculates the sheet until either the *maximum number of iterations* has been reached, or no cell has changed by more than the *maximum change*. As an alternative to a circular reference with iteration, search <u>H</u>elp for 'Goal Seek'.

Excel can only warn you about one circular reference at a time. Therefore one circular reference, even if it is intentional, will hide the existence of another in the same workbook.

To illustrate a circular reference, enter a SUM formula that includes its own cell, as shown next:

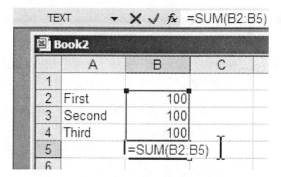

As soon as you enter this, Excel warns:

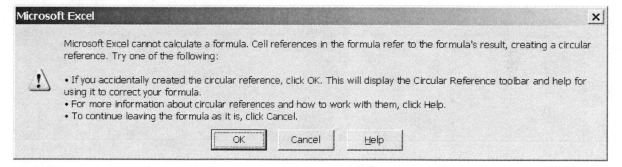

You should click OK and then correct the formula to only sum B2 to B4.

How to locate and remove a circular reference

1. If the Circular Reference toolbar is not displayed, click Customize on the Tools menu, click the Toolbars tab, and then select the Circular Reference check box.

2. On the Circular Reference toolbar, click the first cell in the Navigate Circular Reference box.

3. Review the formula in the cell. If you cannot determine whether the cell is the cause of the circular reference, click the next cell in the Navigate Circular Reference box.

4. Note that the status bar displays the word **Circular**, followed by a reference to one of the cells contained in the circular reference. If the word **Circular** appears without a cell reference, the active worksheet does not contain the circular reference.

Ready		Circular: B4

5. Continue to review and correct the circular reference until the status bar no longer displays the word Circular.

6. When the Circular Reference toolbar appears, tracer arrows appear that point out the cells that depend on the formula.

7. You can move between cells in a circular reference by double-clicking the tracer arrows.

3.1.2 Check your knowledge (*answers on page 169*)

1. How can you detect when a workbook has a circular reference?

2. How can you find a circular reference?

3. What could be a circular reference be intentionally used for?

3.1.3 Identify array (matrix) formulas.

An *array* formula produces multiple results or operates on a group of arguments that are arranged in rows and columns. An array range shares a common formula. Lotus refers to these as *matrix* formulas.

Array formulas can simplify a spreadsheet by replacing several different formulas with a single array formula. They can also help protect against accidental changes within areas. If you try to edit any cell other than the top left corner cell, you get an error message 'You cannot change part of an array'. To delete an array formula, you must select all its cells.

Identify them by the presence of braces (curly brackets) in the formula bar, for example {=B1*B2}. Excel provides no method in Edit > Find to search for array formulas.

The following example from the Excel Help calculates the total value of an array of stock prices and shares, without using a row of cells to calculate and display the individual values for each stock. Type into cell B5 the formula =SUM(B2:D2*B3:D3) and press Ctrl+Shift+Enter to enter it. The array formula multiplies Shares and Price for each stock, and adds the results together. If you press Ctrl+` to display the formulas, the braces do not show in the cell; they only appear in the formula bar.

B5	▾	fx	{=SUM(B2:C2*B3:C3)}	
	A	B	C	D
1		Lorem	Ipsum	
2	Shares	500	300	
3	Price	10	15	
4				
5	Total value	9500		
6				

3.1.3 Check your knowledge (*answers on page 169*)

How would you recognise an array formula?

Skill set: 3.2 Error Identification

3.2.1   Identify missing input values.

You can identify missing input values by checking for empty precedent cells. A *precedent* is a cell that is referred to by the current cell. If the precedent cell is empty, a required input value may be missing.

For some purposes, you may need to explicitly enter a zero in an input cell rather than assuming a blank will be treated the same as a zero. This screenshot shows that the AVERAGE function ignores blank cells:

	B13	▾	fx	=AVERAGE(B4:B9)
	A	B	C	
1	Difference between SUM and AVERAGE			
2				
3	Item	Value		
4	1	126		
5	2			
6	3	234		
7	4	546		
8	5			
9	6	678		
10				
11	Sum	1584		
12	Sum/6	264		
13	Average	396		

This average of 264 is calculated from the SUM divided by 6.

This 396 result is from the Excel AVERAGE function

A cell with no precedents is expected to be either an input that is used in other calculations, or a label like a date or descriptive text. If you see a cell displayed in such a way as to suggest that it is the result of a calculation but it is in fact a direct input, a formula may have been overtyped - accidentally or deliberately - by a constant.

Some auditing and visualisation tools display a drill-down map of precedents at all levels so as to answer the question 'where did that number come from?'

Excel 2002 and later may display a green triangle in a cell, and a screen tip 'The formula in this cell refers to cells that are currently empty'. For more, see Appendix A on Error Checking on page 158.

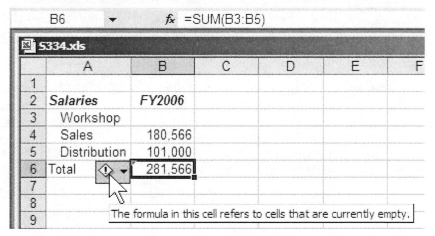

One of the key skills in understanding the logic of a spreadsheet is to be able to trace the chain of calculation. You can select the direct precedents of a cell by double-clicking on the cell. If that does not work for you, on the Tools menu, click Options; on the Edit tab, uncheck Edit directly in cell. An alternative is to press Ctrl+[(opening square bracket). To select precedents at all levels, press Ctrl+{ (opening brace). These actions are also in the menu item Edit > Go To Special:

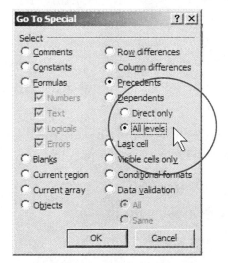

To select all the blank cells in a given region, select the region, use Edit > Go To > Special > Blanks; then use the Tab key to visit each of them.

Excel Help on 'Display the relationships between formulas and cells':

> Excel shows dependencies by tracer arrows. These arrows show the relationship between the active cell and its related cells. Tracer arrows are blue when pointing from a cell that provides data to another cell, and red if a cell contains an error value, such as #DIV/0!.

> To trace cells that provide data to a formula (precedents), select the cell that contains the formula for which you want to find precedent cells.

> To display a tracer arrow to each cell that directly provides data to the active cell, click Trace Precedents on the Formula Auditing toolbar. To identify the next level of cells that provide data to the active cell, click Trace Precedents again. This is how they look:

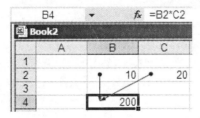

> To remove tracer arrows one level at a time, starting with the precedent cell farthest away from the active cell, click Remove Precedent Arrows. To remove another level of tracer arrows, click the button again.

| Ctrl+[(opening bracket) | Select all cells directly referenced by formulas in the selection. Press F5 and Enter to return to the starting cell. |
| Ctrl+Shift+{ (opening brace) | Select all cells directly or indirectly referenced by formulas in the selection. Press F5 and Enter to return to the starting cell. |

3.2.1 Check your knowledge (*answers on page 169*)

1. How would you check whether a formula was missing input values?

2. Open the file **s3errors.xls**[7] and check for missing inputs on the sheet *Inputs.*

---

[7] Download the example workbooks from http://www.sysmod.com/sbp

3.2.2   Identify cells with missing dependents.

A *dependent* is a cell that refers to the current cell. A cell with no dependents is a final result.

If you see a cell displayed in such a way as to suggest that it is used in a calculation but in fact is not, a formula elsewhere may be omitting this cell reference. For example, it may be a figure in a column that should be included in a total. The picture below shows a total that looks too low. It is only obvious because there are so few cells. In large spreadsheets this will not be obvious.

If we select cell B6 and click the Trace Dependents button on the auditing toolbar, Excel draws a blue arrow from B6 to its dependent B10.

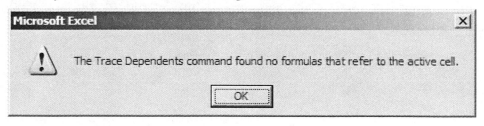

If we try that button on cell B4, we get an alert:

The auditing tools on page 176 can list and highlight formulas with no dependents and show formulas with inconsistent numbers of dependent cells.

The following table shows both toolbar buttons and shortcut keys to find cells that depend on the active cell.

	To trace formulas that reference a particular cell (dependents), select the cell for which you want to identify the dependent cells.
	To display a tracer arrow to each cell that is dependent on the active cell, click Trace Dependents on the Formula Auditing toolbar. To identify the next level of cells that depend on the active cell, click Trace Dependents again.
Ctrl+] (closing bracket)	Select cells that contain formulas that directly reference the active cell. Press F5 and Enter to return to the starting cell.
Ctrl+Shift+} (closing brace)	Select cells that contain formulas that directly or indirectly reference the active cell. Press F5 and Enter to return to the starting cell.
	To remove tracer arrows one level at a time, starting with the dependent cell farthest away from the active cell, click Remove Dependent Arrows. To remove another level of tracer arrows, click the button again.

3.2.2 Check your knowledge (*answers on page 170*)

1. How can you check whether a cell has dependents?

2. Open the file **s3errors.xls** and check for missing dependents on the sheet *Depends*.

<u>CATEGORY: 3 Calculation Skill set: 3.2 Error Identification</u>

3.2.3   Use information functions: ISERROR, ISNA.

ISERROR and *ISNA* are functions you can use to test whether a cell contains an error value. When a cell has an error value, other cells that refer to that cell for calculations will in turn display the same error value. That effect is called *error propagation.*

Use ISERROR or ISNA to control error propagation. It can be used to prevent #N/A displays where missing or invalid inputs are expected and tolerated. But it could also hide error displays that should be seen. Section 3.2.4 on page 63 describes how to *suppress* #DIV/0 displays, and section 3.3.2 on page 71 to *correct* error values.

For example, to show a zero for any error value resulting from dividing C5 by C4, use: `=IF(ISERROR(C5/C4),0,C5/C4)`.

To hide a result that is in error without suppressing error propagation, use conditional formatting. To format a cell (eg, C6) so that any error value is invisible, use **Format > Con**d**itional formatting, Condition 1** is **Formula Is** `=ISERROR($C$6)`, click **Format,** and choose white in the **Color** list. Be aware that auditing software that detects white font on a white background will be suspicious of this and highlight this technique as a possible indicator of intentional deception. See *Reveal Hidden Data* on page 103.

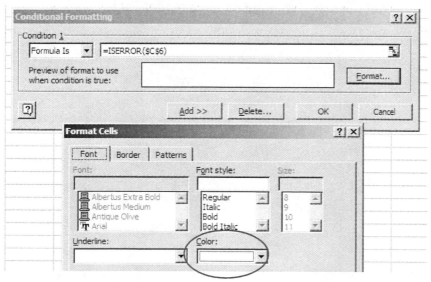

To learn more, search <u>H</u>elp for these functions:

Function	Returns TRUE if
ISERR	Value refers to any error value except #N/A.
ISERROR	Value refers to any error value (#N/A, #VALUE!, #REF!, #DIV/0!, #NUM!, #NAME?, or #NULL!).
ISNA	Value refers to the #N/A (value not available) error value
ISBLANK	Value refers to an empty cell.
ISLOGICAL	Value refers to a logical value
ISNONTEXT	Value refers to any item that is not text. (Note that this function returns TRUE if value refers to a blank cell.)
ISNUMBER	Value refers to a number.
ISREF	Value refers to a reference.
ISTEXT	Value refers to text.

3.2.3 Check your knowledge (*answers on page 170*)

1. What is the risk in hiding an error display?

2. Open the file **s3errors.xls**. On the sheet *Displays*, clear the contents of cell C12. Change cell C13 to use a formula to hide the error.

CATEGORY: 3 Calculation Skill set: 3.2 Error Identification

3.2.4   Suppress display of #DIV/0! values.

Division by zero is not a valid operation in mathematics. Often it happens when the cell you are dividing by (the divisor) is empty. For example, percentage calculations may show *division by zero* errors for periods for which data are not yet available.

	A	B	C	D	E	F
	C6	▾	*fx* =C5/C4			

S331.xls

	A	B	C	D	E	F
1						
2	Month	Jan	Feb	Mar	*Qtr1*	
3						
4	Sales	10000			*10000*	
5	Salaries	1000	1000	1000	*3000*	
6	Salaries as % of Sales	⚠ ▾	#DIV/0!	#DIV/0!	*30%*	
7						
8			The formula or function used is dividing by zero or empty cells.			
9						

If there is no value yet, or the divisor really is zero, you may wish to suppress the display of the error.

You can either keep the error result and hide it, or change it to a non error value.

If you keep the error value, it will be propagated to any other formulas that refer to it. Where it is a final result, you may prefer simply to hide it until a non-zero divisor is available. To hide its display, use a conditional format as described on page 61 to set the font colour to be the same as the background.

If you change the result to a zero, ensure that this will not cause incorrect subsequent calculations that may misrepresent results.

If you change the result to a blank text value, ensure that this does not cause undesirable results with dependent formulas. Text values like a space or a dash can cause errors in calculations that expect a numeric value. To change the result, use an IF function as shown below.

In the following example, C5 contains the dividend (the number being divided, the numerator) and C4 contains the divisor (the number doing the division, the denominator), so the formula is =C5/C4.

1) Test for the divisor being zero:

   a) To show a blank, use =IF(C4=0,"",C5/C4)

   b) To show a dash, use =IF(C4=0,"-",C5/C4)

   c) To show zero, use =IF(C4=0,0,C5/C4)

   d) The display of zeroes can be suppressed by unselecting <u>T</u>ools > <u>O</u>ptions > View > Window Options, <u>Z</u>ero values.

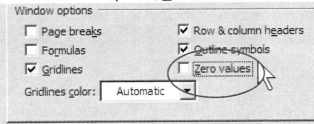

2) In logical tests, Excel treats zero values as FALSE, and non-zero as TRUE. So you could express the formula as =IF(C4,C5/C4,0). However, not every future user will understand that shortcut.

3) To show a blank text value for *any* error result, use the ISERROR function: =IF(ISERROR(C5/C4),"",C5/C4). However, this may hide problems other than simple division by zero. Do not hide the error display if the user needs to know when some data is missing.

To suppress error values when printing, on the File menu, click Page Setup, and then click the Sheet tab. Under Print in the Cell errors as box, click **<blank>**, **- -**, or **#N/A**.

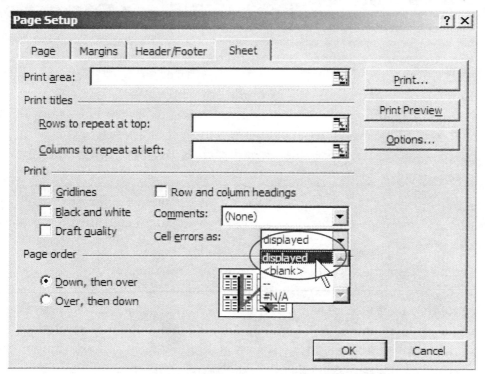

Check what causes the errors before you hide them. You will probably be better off fixing the errors rather than 'sweeping them under the carpet'.

3.2.4 Check your knowledge (*answers on page 171*)

1. What is the risk in displaying a zero rather than #DIV/0?

2. Open the file **s3errors.xls**. On the sheet *Div0*, clear the contents of cell C4. Change cell C5 to use a formula to hide the error.

Skill set: 3.3 Error Correction

| 3.3.1 | Correct relative, absolute and mixed cell references. |

A *relative* cell reference, such as A1, in a formula, describes the relative position of the cell that contains the formula and the cell the reference refers to. For example, the formula =B1 in cell C1 means 'take the value from the cell on the left'. (This is further explained on page 68.) If you copy the formula across rows or down columns, the reference automatically adjusts.

An *absolute* cell reference in a formula, such as $A$1, always refers to a cell in a specific location. If you copy the formula across rows or down columns, the absolute reference does not adjust.

A *mixed* reference has either an absolute column and relative row, or absolute row and relative column. An absolute column reference takes the form $A1, $B1, and so on. An absolute row reference takes the form A$1, B$1, and so on. If you copy such a formula, the relative reference is changed, and the absolute reference does not change. If you are not sure about these, search <u>H</u>elp for 'About cell and range references' and 'The difference between relative and absolute references'.

To create these different kinds of references, either type the dollar sign where required, or use function key F4 while pointing to a cell to cycle among the four combinations. This table shows the results of pressing F4 four times:

Type:	*press F4 once*	*press F4 again*	*press F4 again*	*press F4 again*
=a6*b4	=a6*$B$4	=a6*B$4	=a6*$B4	=a6*B4

A range name may be a more understandable way of referring to an absolute cell address. Range names are described on page 36.

To find and correct mistakes in the use of relative, absolute and mixed cell references, show the formulas and examine them carefully, as described in the next example.

Show formulas to examine references

The following worksheet is intended to calculate 30% profit on sales for each month. It is obviously wrong as the profit exceeds sales. In real life, errors are not always so obvious, unfortunately.

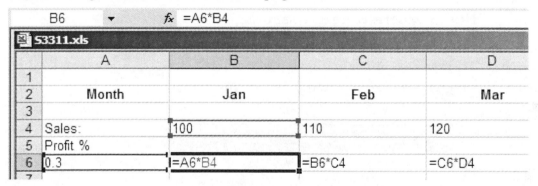

To switch between displaying formulas and their values on a worksheet, press Ctrl+` (backtick or grave accent, described on page 143):

	A	B	C	D
1				
2	Month	Jan	Feb	Mar
3				
4	Sales:	100	110	120
5	Profit %			
6	0.3	=A6*B4	=B6*C4	=C6*D4
7				

You can then infer that the formula in B6 was copied to the right, and that the reference to A6 should have been $A6 so that the reference to column A would not change in the copies.

To avoid copy & paste errors when updating blocks of formulas, use a single formula for an entire row. In other words, don't change formula part way across a row to cope with something that occurs in that time period. Use separate rows for each case.

R1C1 style

The apparent changes in relative formulas when they are copied are simply a consequence of how the A1 reference style makes them appear. View a worksheet in R1C1 style (Tools > Options > General tab > Settings, R1C1 reference style) to understand better how Excel stores the formulas. It will show you that copying a formula copies it exactly in its R1C1 style. RC[-1] refers to the cell in the same row, one column left. R[-2]C refers to the cell two rows above in the same column. (More on page 143).

R6C2	▼	*fx* =RC[-1]*R[-2]C		
S3311.xls				
	1	2	3	4
1				
2	Month	Jan	Feb	Mar
3				
4	Sales:	100	110	120
5	Profit %			
6	0.3	=RC[-1]*R[-2]C	=RC[-1]*R[-2]C	=RC[-1]*R[-2]C
7				

Intersections: where ranges meet

Other sections in this book refer to intersecting ranges, so we describe them here for reference. An intersection is a cell where two ranges intersect. For example, the cell C3 is at the intersection of C1:C5 and A3:E3 as shown here:

C3		▼	*fx* 33		
References.xls					
	A	B	C	D	E
1			31		
2			32		
3	13	23	33	43	53
4			34		
5			35		

If the range C1:C5 is given the name *MyCol* and the range A3:E3 is given the name *MyRow*, then we can refer to the intersection of that row and that column by using the two names separated by a space, which is the *explicit intersection* operator. For example, we can place a formula in A1 to refer to C3 as follows:

```
=MyCol MyRow
```

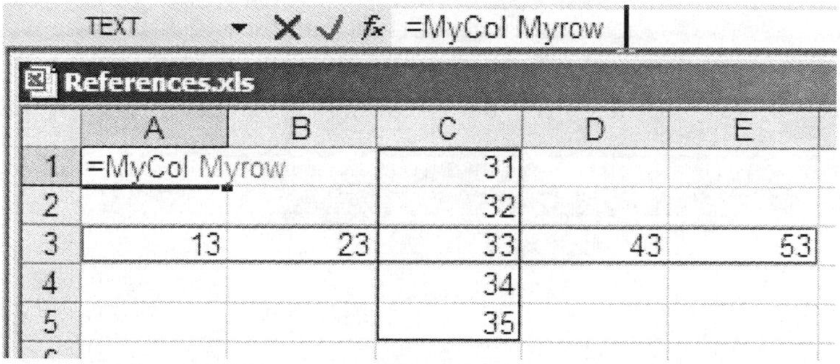

While entering the formula, Excel places coloured borders around the ranges being referred to as shown above. On entering the formula, it refers to C3:

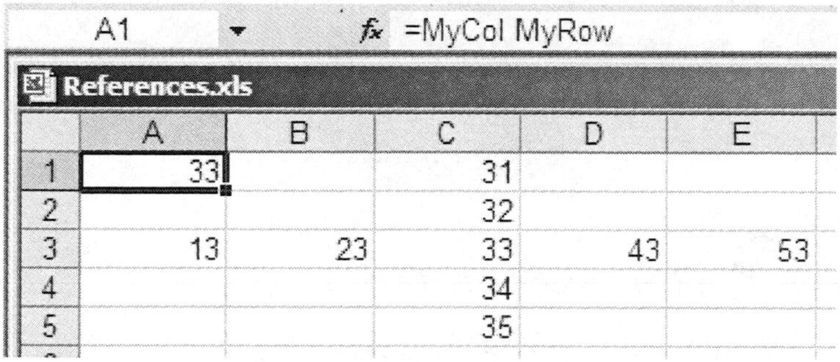

The space character *explicitly* defines the two ranges where Excel has to determine the intersection. If there is no intersection, the #NULL! error is returned, as described on page 77. If you only use one range name, Excel uses an *implicit intersection* of the row or column, of the cell into which you are entering the formula, with the column or row of the range name. Thus entering =MyRow in B7 would return the intersection of column B with the range A3:E3, which is cell B3, as shown here:

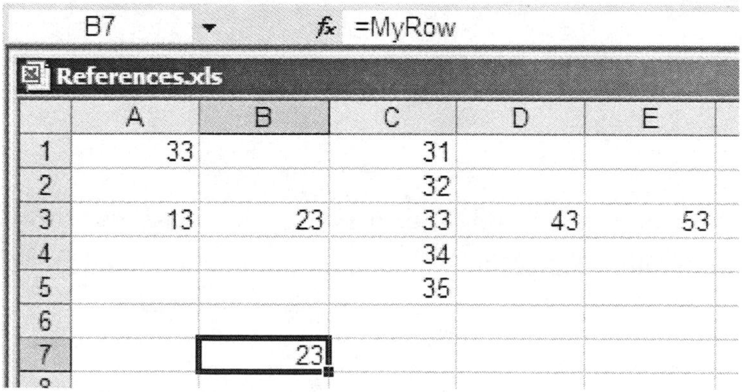

Entering =MyCol in cell G4 would return the intersection of row 4 with the range C1:C5, which is cell C4, as shown here:

| G4 | ▼ | f_x =MyCol |

References.xls

	A	B	C	D	E	F	G
1	33		31				
2			32				
3	13	23	33	43	53		
4			34				34
5			35				
6							
7		23					

That is why names that refer to a range of cells can be used in formulas, Excel figures out which row or column is required from this implicit intersection.

3.3.1 Check your knowledge (*answers on page 171*)

1. Open the file **s3errors.xls**. On the sheet *AbsRel*, correct the cell references.

2. Create a two-way multiplication table where each cell contains the value in the left column times the value in the top row, for example:

multtable.xls

	A	B	C	D	E
1	Multiplication Table				
2		-1	2	5	10
3	2.204				
4	2.54				
5	3.1416				
6	5				
7	9.99				

Begin by entering a formula in cell B3, and then copy it across and down to cell E7. Check that the results are correct.

CATEGORY: 3 Calculation Skill set: 3.3 Error Correction

> **3.3.2   Identify and correct error values indicated by # signs.**

This is a large section, as we shall discuss each error value separately.

3.3.2.1 Identify error values.

In Excel, on the Edit menu, choose Go To, (shortcut: Ctrl+G or F5), click Special (this is only available if the worksheet is unprotected), select Formulas, select only Errors, and click OK.

How to trace the cause of an error

 A green triangle in the upper-left corner of a cell indicates an error in the formula in the cell.

In Excel 2002 and later, if you select the cell, the Trace Error button appears. Click the arrow next to the button for a list of options.

- Help on this error

- Show calculation steps

- Ignore error

- Edit in Formula Bar

- Show error checking options

- Show auditing toolbar

Search Help for 'Find and correct errors in formulas'. To get detailed help on each error value, search Help for ' Correct a ##### error', substituting the name of the error value for the hashes in that example.

3.3.2.2 Correct a ##### display

This is a display feature rather than an error value. It occurs when a column is not wide enough, or a negative number is formatted as a date or time.

8,000.00
########

(a) Increase the width of the column

8,000.00
10,000.00

(b) Shrink the contents to fit the column - on the Format menu, click Cells, click the Alignment tab, and then select the Shrink to fit check box

(c) Apply a different number format

(d) Decrease the number of decimal places after the decimal point

(e) Reduce the font size.

3.3.2.3 Correct a #VALUE! Error

#VALUE! is most commonly the result of an arithmetical calculation that refers directly to a cell that contains text.

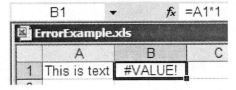

On the other hand, functions that operate on ranges such as SUM ignore text values included in the range. If the cell referred to *appears* to be blank, it may be because a user pressed the space bar in a mistaken attempt to clear a cell. A space character is not visible but is nonetheless text. (It would be nice to have an option in spreadsheet software that shows some other character for spaces, as word processors can do).

You can use Edit > Replace (shortcut: Ctrl+H) to find all instances of a single space in a cell (check the box Match Entire Cell Contents) and replace it by 0 (zero). The delete key clears the contents and Edit > Clear > All clears formats as well.

Where you have numbers entered as text, you can use the VALUE() function to convert them to numbers.

#VALUE! can also be returned by a LOOKUP function where the column index number is less than 1.

3.3.2.4 Correct a #NAME? Error

This occurs when the spreadsheet does not recognize text in a formula as being a valid cell address, range name, or function name.

It can be caused by using a function that is part of an add-in, without the add-in being loaded.

If the text is a range name that should exist, then define it. On the Insert menu, point to Name, and then click Define. If the name is not listed, add the name by using the Define command. You may discover, however, that you have simply misspelled the name, in which case you edit the formula to correct it. Here, *taxrate* is not yet defined:

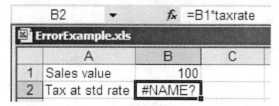

If the text is a function name, seek Help in the program for functions to get the correct spelling. A useful habit is to enter function names in lowercase. A recognised function name will appear in uppercase in the formula bar, so where you see lower-case is the invalid function name, as in summ below.

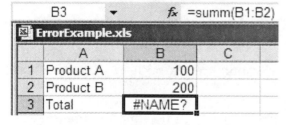

To enter text in a formula, enclosed the text in double quotation marks, for example:
=IF(X11=Y12,"Same","Different")

Other possible causes are omitting a colon (:) in a range reference, or referencing another sheet not enclosed in single quotation marks.

Excel has a workbook option named Accept labels in formulas but we discourage its use as it may give rise to more confusion than assistance. It allows the use of cell text labels as an automatic range name. These do not appear in the range name list. As an alternative, software tools like the *Spreadsheet Detective* and *EXChecker* create annotations in spreadsheets based on the row and column labels.

3.3.2.5 Correct a #N/A Error

This occurs when a value is not available to a function or formula.

You can enter #N/A or =NA( ) in those cells where data is not yet available. Formulas that refer to those cells will then return #N/A instead of attempting to calculate a value. This may be done intentionally to indicate to the user that they have not completed all inputs.

Other causes are:

- Giving an inappropriate value for the `lookup_value` argument in the HLOOKUP, LOOKUP, MATCH, or VLOOKUP spreadsheet function (more information for these is on page 96).

- Using the VLOOKUP, HLOOKUP, or MATCH function to locate an approximate value in an unsorted table. To find an exact match in an unsorted table, set the `range_lookup` argument to FALSE. See 3.3.10 on page 96 for examples of how to correct #N/A values from lookup functions.

- The MATCH spreadsheet function contains a `match_type` argument that specifies the order the list must be sorted in to find a match. If the function returns #N/A because it cannot find a match, try changing the `match_type` argument. To find an exact match, set the `match_type` argument to 0.

- Using an argument in an array formula that is not the same number of rows or columns as the range that contains the array formula.

- Omitting one or more required arguments from a built-in or custom spreadsheet function.

- Using a custom spreadsheet function that is not available; make sure the workbook that contains the spreadsheet function is open and the function is working properly.

- Running a macro that enters a function that returns #N/A.

3.3.2.6 Correct a #REF! Error

This occurs when a cell reference is not valid.

Most commonly #REF! is caused by deleting cells referred to by other formulas, or pasting moved cells over cells referred to by other formulas.

Before:

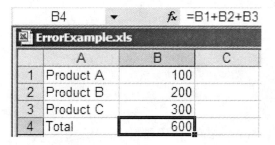

After deleting row 2:

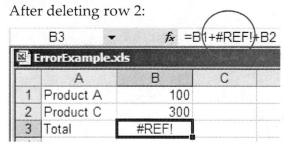

If you notice the error soon after a deletion, you may be able to Undo (shortcut: Ctrl+Z); if not, you may be able to revert to a previously saved backup.

Other causes:

- Using a column index number in a LOOKUP function that is greater than the number of columns in the lookup table

- Linking to a Dynamic Data Exchange (DDE) topic such as *system* that is not available

- Running a macro that enters a function that returns #REF!

3.3.2.7   Correct a #NUM! error

This occurs with invalid numeric values in a formula or function. Most commonly #NUM! is caused by using an unacceptable argument in a function that requires a numeric argument.

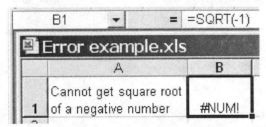

Other causes:

- Using a spreadsheet function that iterates, such as IRR or RATE, and the function cannot find a result

- Entering a formula that produces a number that is too large or too small to be represented in your spreadsheet program

3.3.2.8   Correct a #NULL! error

This occurs when you specify an intersection of two areas that do not intersect. The intersection operator (described on page 68) is a space between references. A space is invisible and therefore easily overlooked.

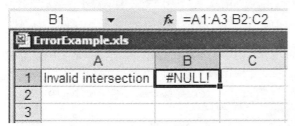

- To refer to a contiguous range of cells, use a colon (:) to separate the reference to the first cell in the range from the reference to the last cell in the range. For example, SUM(B1:B10) refers to the range from cell B1 to cell B10 inclusive.

- To refer to two areas that don't intersect, use the union operator, the comma (,). For example, if the formula sums two ranges, make sure a comma separates the two ranges, eg:

  SUM(B1:B10,C1:C10)

- An intentional intersection can be created if you have, for example, a row range named *Sales* and a column range named *East*. The intersection formula =East Sales designates that Microsoft Excel should find and return the value in the cell at the intersection of the two ranges.

3.3.2 Check your knowledge (*answers on page 173*)

Open the file **s3errors.xls**. On the sheet *Errors*, identify and correct all the errors.

3.3.3   Correct inconsistencies in a pattern of formulas.

An *inconsistency* arises when one formula in a block of cells is different from those in its neighbourhood. Possible causes are:

1. A user is typing repeated formulas individually rather than creating copies (or *clones*) using either copy & paste or the drag or fill commands. Because of all the repeated typing, they forget some references in some formulas that they include in others.

2. A user types a constant into a cell in a mistaken attempt to correct a formula.

3. A formula omits adjacent nonempty cells.

Excel 2002 and later helps to some extent by flagging inconsistent cells in a block with a green triangle in the upper left corner, see on page 158.

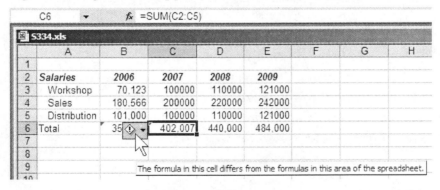

Finding these requires visually scanning the entire spreadsheet. Visualization tools (see Appendix C on page 163) can speedily detect anomalies in patterns of formulas.

In Excel 2000 and later you can select the range you want to test and then use the Edit > Go To > Special menu command with these options:

Row Differences: Cells in the same row as the active cell, whose contents are different from the active cell. Shortcut: Ctrl+\

Column Differences: Cells in the same column as the active cell, whose contents are different from the active cell. Shortcut: Ctrl+Shift+|

If more than one cell is found, they are shaded as a multiple selection and you can use the Tab key to visit each of them.

An example follows.

A5	▼	=	=SUM(A2:A4)			C5	▼	=	=SUM(C2:C3)

	A	B	C	D	E
1	Totals of rows 2 to 4				
2	12	22	32	42	
3	13	23	33	43	
4	14	24	34	44	
5	39	69	65	129	
6					
7	Go To Special			? ×	
8					
9	Select				
10	○ Comments		◉ Row differences		

The formulas should sum rows 2 to 4, use <u>E</u>dit > <u>G</u>o to > <u>S</u>pecial to check for differences.

	A	B	C	D
1	Totals of rows 2 to 4			
2	12	22	32	42
3	13	23	33	43
4	14	24	34	44
5	39	69	65	129

This is the one it finds, which refers to C2:C3. The other formulas refer to A2:A4, B2:B4, and D2:D4.

Example of a spreadsheet colouring tool

Many auditing tools (list on page 163) produce maps that highlight inconsistent formulas by using colour. This example is taken from *SpACE – Spreadsheet Auditing, HM Revenue and Customs*. A cell in the bottom right showing UF is circled below, on screen it is highlighted in red. UF means Unique Formula; this total formula was mistyped and so is different from all the others in the worksheet.

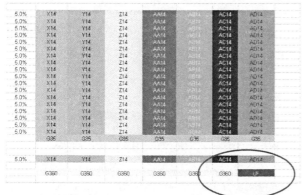

3.3.3 Check your knowledge (*answers on page 174*)

Open the file **s3errors.xls**. On the sheet *Inconsistent*, identify and correct all the errors.

> ### 3.3.4   Correct mistakes in totals caused by inserting, deleting rows and columns.

Rows or columns *inserted* at the edges of areas currently referred to by formulas may not be included automatically in those formulas. *Deleting* rows or columns in ranges referred to by formulas may cause reference errors in those formulas.

If the area is referred to by its address, eg, =SUM(B3:B5), you can see on reading the formula whether it is missing a row or column that you see from the context should be included. On the other hand, if it is referred to by a range name, eg, =SUM(Sales), then it is more easily overlooked unless you remember to check the definition of the range name.

To create a total of rows that is safely expandable, provide an extra empty row above and below. Then include them in the total so that insertions of more rows, at either of these, will be included. A similar method applies to columns.

As an exercise, create a worksheet using the data below.

	B6	▼	*fx* =SUM(B3:B5)	
InsertTest.xls				
	A		B	
1				
2	Salaries		FY2006	
3	Workshop		70,000	
4	Sales		100,000	
5	Distribution		100,000	
6	Total		270,000	
7				

Save it as **InsertTest.xls**. B6 contains the formula =SUM(B3:B5) which is correct at the moment. Now insert a new row at row 3. The formula at what is now B7 will therefore read =SUM(B4:B6). Type *Management* into A3 and *20000* into B3 and you will see that the value in B3 is not included in the total. If you are using Excel 2002 or later, you should also see a green triangle in B7 and a screen tip that tells you 'The formula in this cell refers to a range that has additional numbers adjacent to it':

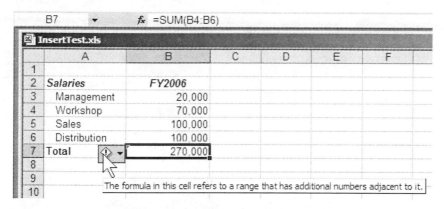

Save this spreadsheet as **InsertAtTop.xls** and close the file. It is not needed again in this exercise, but you might wish to refer to it later.

What happens if you insert an empty row just above a total? That depends on an application setting in Excel, *Extend list formats and formulas*, that sometimes – but not always – automatically copies cell formats and formulas, and adjusts total formulas, when you add rows at the end of a list. To be extended, formats and formulas must appear in at least three of the five list rows preceding the new row. This is an *application* setting, so it applies to all workbooks opened after it is enabled. Try this exercise:

The Phantom Formula Fixer

Open the file **InsertTest.xls** from the exercise above. On the Tools menu, click Options, and on the Edit tab, **uncheck** Extend list formats and formulas

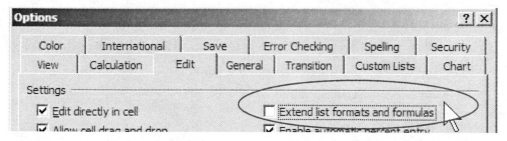

B6 contains the formula =SUM(B3:B5). Now insert a new row at row 6. The formula at what is now B7 will still read =SUM(B3:B5). Type *Management* into A6 and *20000* into B6 and you will see that the value in B6 is not included in the total. If you are using Excel 2002 or later, you should also see a green triangle in B7 and a screen tip that tells you 'The formula in this cell refers to a range that has additional numbers adjacent to it':

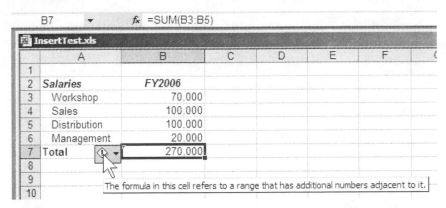

Close the file without saving it. Re-open the file **InsertTest.xls**. On the Tools menu, click Options, and on the Edit tab, **check** Extend list formats and formulas

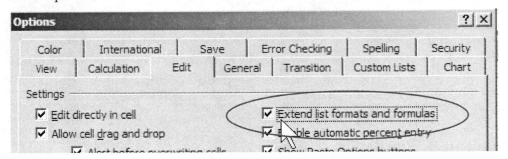

B6 contains the formula =SUM(B3:B5). Now insert a new row at row 6. The formula at what is now B7 will still read =SUM(B3:B5). Enter *Management* into A6. Watch carefully as you enter *20000* into B6. You might see Excel select cell B7, change the formula, and then move back up to B6. The total is now correct. Check the formula in B7 and it has been changed to =SUM(B3:B6). Do not rely on this behaviour; always check that totals refer to the correct range of cells.

To check for formulas omitting rows or columns

To detect that all the data are correctly included in totals, do one of these:

- Visit each total cell and read its formula and check that it includes the whole range required. This may be well beyond what is visible on the screen, so you may have to scroll around.

- Use Excel 2002 or later that has error detection features. A green triangle (see Trace Error on page 71) in the corner of a cell appears if an unusual pattern is detected. See the illustration below.

- Use a spreadsheet auditing tool that draws your attention to data just outside the range of totals.

Removing a cell – that is, deleting a whole row, column, or cell, can cause a #REF error if any formula referred to the deleted cell. To avoid this, clear the cell using the delete key or <u>E</u>dit > Cle<u>a</u>r > <u>A</u>ll, rather than removing the cell from the structure of the worksheet.

When you delete a row or column at the end of a SUM range, Excel automatically adjusts the range in the function.

3.3.4 Check your knowledge (*answers on page 174*)

Open the file **s3errors.xls**. On the sheet *InsRow*, insert a new row at row 11, enter 100 in B11,C11,D11 and then adjust the formulas to obtain the correct totals.

3.3.5   Correct grand totals that double-count subtotals.

A SUM total may accidentally include other SUM subtotals inside it.

Instead of using SUM, use the SUBTOTAL function. It has the form:

`SUBTOTAL(function_num,ref1,ref2,...)`

`Function_num` is a number from 1 to 11 that specifies which function to use in calculating subtotals within a list. The number 9 means SUM; search <u>H</u>elp for 'Subtotal' for more information. This function is extended in Excel 2003.

SUBTOTAL has these useful features:

- If there are other `=SUBTOTAL` formulas within `ref1, ref2,...` (or nested subtotals), these nested subtotals are ignored to avoid double counting.

- SUBTOTAL will ignore any hidden rows that result from a list being filtered. This is when you want to subtotal only the visible data from a filtered list.

This shows the different results of the SUM and SUBTOTAL functions:

subtotals.xls

	A	B	C	D
1	Totals example		Simple SUM	Subtotal
2				
3	Dept A			
4		Product 1	100	100
5		Product 2	100	100
6		Product 3	100	100
7	Subtotal A		300	300
8				
9	Dept B			
10		Product 4	100	100
11		Product 5	100	100
12		Product 6	100	100
13	Subtotal B		300	300
14				
15	Grand total		1200	600

Here is the same sheet in Formula View:

	A	B	C	D
	subtotals.xls			
1	Totals example		Simple SUM	Subtotal
2				
3	*Dept A*			
4		Product 1	100	100
5		Product 2	100	100
6		Product 3	100	100
7	*Subtotal A*		=SUM(C4:C6)	=SUBTOTAL(9,D4:D6)
8				
9	*Dept B*			
10		Product 4	100	100
11		Product 5	100	100
12		Product 6	100	100
13	*Subtotal B*		=SUM(C10:C12)	=SUBTOTAL(9,D10:D12)
14				
15	*Grand total*		=SUM(C4:C13)	=SUBTOTAL(9,D4:D13)

Reported cases of double-counting totals

http://www.gao.gov/decisions/bidpro/292555.htm   October 10, 2003

'Our review of the record, including Emerson's computer-generated spreadsheets, confirms that the price at spreadsheet cell number D159 (for electrical work) was not included in the subtotal at cell number D160. Based on the format of the spreadsheet, it is clear that the $3,702,025 price at cell number D159 was intended to be included in the firm's subtotal price.'

Also at: http://www.pubklaw.com/rd/gao/2003/B-2925552.html

http://oig.hhs.gov/oas/reports/region4/40202016.pdf

'The FY 1999 Medicare/Medicaid crossover log contained calculation errors, resulting in the log being overstated by $38,240. The hospital inadvertently included some cells in a subtotal and also added them a second time in the grand total. In addition, the hospital inadvertently omitted one subtotal from the grand total. These errors resulted in the summary totals being overstated. '

3.3.5 Check your knowledge (*answers on page 175*)

Open the file **s3errors.xls**. On the sheet *Budget07*, find and correct the double-counted totals.

3.3.6   Correct mismatched cross-check totals.

Create cross-check totals for validation. This is a good basic accounting practice. (Although a spreadsheet is not a substitute for a real bookkeeping package. After all, how many accounting packages allow the user to change the calculation methods?) It gives the assurance that, eg, all the data included in the total down is also included in the total across, or the total of debits equals the total of credits.

In the following example, F11 calculates the profit in the same way as the other columns (sales minus costs), and F12 is the sum of B11:E11. The formula in A13 is showing a blank result because the totals agree.

A13		f_x =IF(F12=F11,"","Cross-check sum of profit row is different!")					

CrossCheck.xls

	A	B	C	D	E	F	G
1	Forecast						
2		2006	2007	2008	2009	Total	
3	Sales						
4	Dept. A	38308	42139	46353	50988	177787	
5	Dept. B	1000	1000	1000	1000	4000	
6	Costs						
7	Direct costs	4900	5000	5100	5234	20234	
8	Overheads	18122	21000	19234	18468	76824	
9	Biennial		10000		10000	20000	
10							
11	Profit	16286	7139	23019	18286	**64729**	
12					Check:	64729	
13							
14							

Even where the numbers do not represent quantities, you can still create artificial totals, called *hash totals*. They are used where you wish to check that all the numbers in one place are also present in another place, and an artificial total will differ if some number is missing from the second set. It will not show compensating errors, such as omitting invoice number 1001 and changing invoice number 1000 to 2001.

3.3.6 Check your knowledge (*answers on page 175*)

Open the file **s3errors.xls**. On the sheet *Budget08*, correct the cross-check totals at the bottom right.

CATEGORY: 3 Calculation Skill set: 3.3 Error Correction

3.3.7   Correct mistakes created by incorrect use of automatic sum feature.

Blank cells can cause problems with an automatic feature that selects only the nearest region containing data. This is an example:

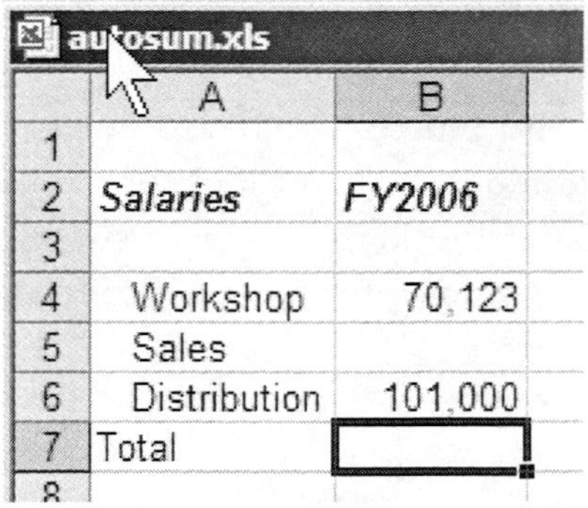

Cell B5 is empty. If you select cell B7 and then <u>double-click</u> the AutoSum button Σ ▾ , it enters the formula =SUM(B6). That is because it stopped looking up the column when it found the first non-numeric entry.

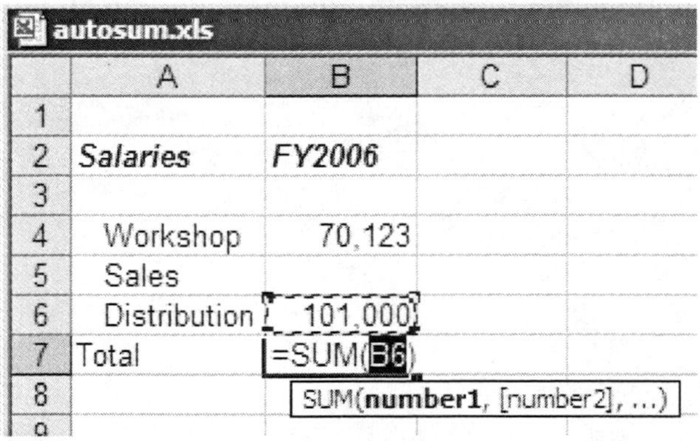

To avoid this, one can enter a zero into every empty cell before performing the autosum.

The correct usage is to <u>single</u>-click the button, carefully check the suggested range, and change it if necessary before pressing Enter.

To check existing formulas that refer to ranges, examine the extreme ends of the ranges to be sure that all and only the intended cells are included.

Other automatic features can catch people unawares. The following story cautions users about the AutoComplete feature:

---

http://catless.ncl.ac.uk/Risks/21.94.html

Yet another case of a program changing your input, Risks Digest 10 Mar 2002.

'I was entering grades in an Excel spreadsheet and realized that although in my notes I had a mix of A's and A-'s, the spreadsheet had changed all the A grades to A-'s. Why? I was entering grades looking at my notes and not the screen. So I typed A- followed by ENTER, then A at which point Excel suggested A- as a possible input. Without looking I pressed ENTER, thus entering A- instead of A. This only works if the longer input precedes the shorter in the original list (i.e., the list you are typing from), since if there is ambiguity about the suggestion, Excel shuts up.'

3.3.7 Check your knowledge (*answers on page 175*)

Open the file **s3errors.xls**. On the sheet *FiveYear*, select the cell C51 which is the total of the first column of numbers. Click the Autosum button <u>once</u> and review the data range. What do you have to be careful of?

3.3.8   Replace linking by cell address with linking by range name between files.

A spreadsheet that provides data for other spreadsheets is termed a *source* spreadsheet. The spreadsheet that links to that data is termed a *target* spreadsheet. Apply a range name to each distinct block of cells in a source spreadsheet that you intend to link to from a target spreadsheet. When entering the external link in the target spreadsheet, refer to the address in the source spreadsheet by its range name rather than by its cell address, eg, C5.

This avoids the problem that arises where:

1. a formula in the target sheet refers to a source cell by address;
2. a user moves the location of the data in the source sheet;
3. the reference in the target sheet is not changed to correspond;
4. as a result data is imported from the wrong location.

Don't do:	`='F:\Topdir1\[source1.xls]Sheet1'!$A$2`
Do this:	`='F:\Topdir1\[source1.xls]Sheet1'!Somename`
or this:	`='F:\Topdir1\source1.xls'!Atest`

To search in a workbook for cells containing links, search for the exclamation mark (!) in formulas. You should maintain documentation of these external links. Auditing tools can also list them.

To get an overview of the linked workbooks, use <u>E</u>dit > Lin<u>k</u>s. The following screen-shot shows the display after clicking the *Check Status* button:

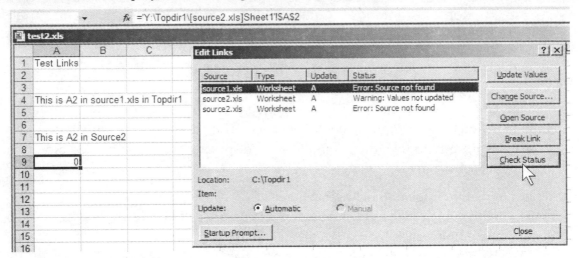

Fraud using linked workbooks

http://www.gre.ac.uk/~cd02/eusprig/2001/AIB_Spreadsheets.htm

Allfirst 'Would not pay the US$ 10,000 for a direct data feed from Reuters to the risk control section'. Instead, they got Rusnak to download his Reuters feed into a spreadsheet. He then substituted links to his private manipulated spreadsheet. The total losses hidden by the fraud were almost US$700M. Rusnak exaggerated bonuses by over half a million dollars. Ray Butler points out in the article above that 'One error in a spreadsheet will subvert all the controls in all the systems feeding into it'. An auditing tool (SpACE) would have found the external links in the key spreadsheet.

3.3.8 Check your knowledge - exercise

1. In a new workbook, enter your name in A1. Save as **Test1.xls**, don't close it.

2. Start a new workbook (shortcut: Ctrl+N), type an equals sign in A1. On the <u>W</u>indow menu select **Test1.xls**, click on cell A1, and press Enter. You should see `=[Test1.xls]Sheet1!$A$1` in the formula bar and the cell should display your name. Save as **Test2.xls** and close.

3. In **Test1.xls**, insert a new row at row 1. Save and close.

4. Re-open **Test2.xls**. If you are asked to update links, click Update. A1 now shows a zero. That is because it is now referring to an empty source cell.

5. Now repeat the above steps this time using a range name:

6. In a new workbook, enter your name in A1. Give that cell a name by typing *Myname* into the Name box.

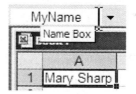

7. Save as **Test3.xls** and close it.

8. Start a new workbook (shortcut: Ctrl+N). In cell A1, enter the formula `=Test3!Myname` and the cell should display your name. Note that the formula bar shows in single quotes the full path and file name of the source data.

9. Save as **Test4.xls** and close.

10. Re-open **Test3.xls**, insert a new row at row 1. Save and close.

11. Re-open **Test4.xls**. If you are asked to update links, click Update. A1 still shows your name because the range name was updated in **Test3** when you inserted a row there.

> **3.3.9   Recognise link references and understand problems caused by changes in linked files.**

A *reference* to a range in another worksheet can be recognised by the exclamation mark (!) in the formula, eg, `=Sheet3!B2`

A reference to a range in another spreadsheet file is enclosed in single quotes (apostrophes) and the source file name is in square brackets ([]), eg,

`='C:\Topdir1\[source1.xls]Sheet1'!$A$2`

Let's look at how Excel stores links in workbooks. The spreadsheet file containing the link is the *target*, and the file containing the linked data is the *source*. If the source file is in the same directory as the target, or below, Excel stores a relative pathname – that is, only the subdirectory and file name is specified, not the full directory path. This is to ensure that when linked workbooks are copied together to a new location, the same relative directory paths apply. However, files in other directories have the full path and file name, including the drive letter, stored. The presence of the drive letter often causes confusion when files are moved to different drives, which could be mapped drives on a server.

For example, take a file called **target.xls** in the directory **C:\test** which links to three source files. The first source **one.xls** is in **C:\test**, the second **two.xls** is in **C:\test\subtest** and the third **three.xls** is in **C:\other**.

- A file in the same directory has no explicit path specified, only the file name. The first link would be stored with a path to **one.xls**.

- A file in a directory below the target's directory has only the subdirectory path specified in the link. The second link would be stored with a path to **subtest\two.xls**.

- A file in any other directory has the full path and file name, including the drive letter, stored. The third link would be stored with a path to **C:\other\three.xls**.

This diagram shows how Excel stores these references internally in the file. In the formula bar, the links will all appear to have the full path and file name.

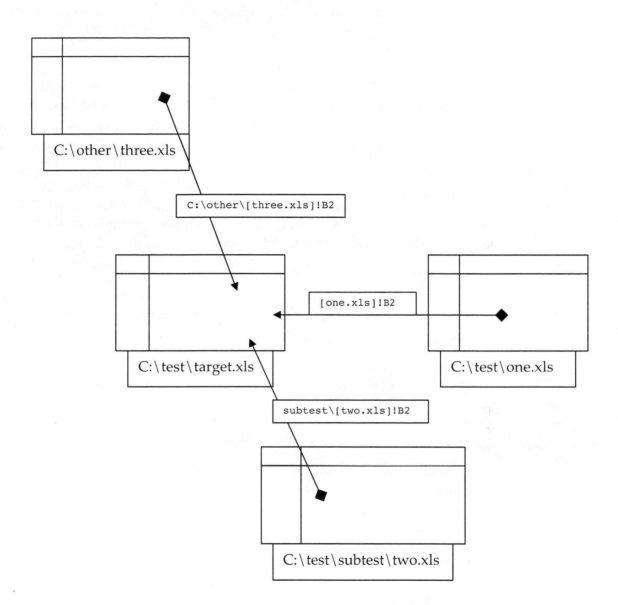

It makes a difference whether the source workbooks are open

If you have all the linked workbooks open at the same time in Excel, you can safely save them under different names or in different locations. Excel will automatically keep the links pointing to the right file. On the other hand, if you change the source file names or locations through operating system commands outside of Excel, the following problems can occur:

- **File name changes**

  If the source file name is changed outside of Excel, the workbook will still hold a name that is no longer valid, and will give an error when it is opened. Another possibility is that after renaming a source workbook, some other workbook could then be renamed to the original source name. This would shift the links to a different workbook.

- **File location changes**

  If a non-relative linked workbook is moved to another location, or deleted, the link is not updated. It will fail when the referring workbook is opened.

- **File layout changes**

  If cells (referred to by cell address rather than range name) are moved or deleted, the referring workbook will pick up data from the originally specified location which will, therefore, be different.

  If the source file layout is changed by deleting *range* or *worksheet* names that are referred to by name, the referring workbook will not find the data.

3.3.9 Check your knowledge - exercise

We recommend you practice this in a similar way to the exercise in the previous section. Create workbooks with links and then try making various changes and observing the results.

Stories about incorrect links

http://www.sao.state.ut.us/reports/03-37.pdf June 30, 2003

Utah State Auditor Department Of Natural Resources Finding And Recommendation; Indirect Cost Rate Calculated Incorrectly (Reportable Condition) 'The indirect cost electronic spreadsheet for Habitat Management direct salaries and benefits, titled "Short Form Method," had a cell that was linked to an incorrect spreadsheet. This resulted in an overstatement of the direct cost base by over $2 million. '

Microsoft knowledgebase articles:

www.microsoft.com/technet/prodtechnol/office/office2000/tips/exlink1.mspx
Create and Manage Links to Other Workbooks in Excel 2000

You can edit linking formulas to use UNC names, such as \\myserver\myshare, instead of drive letters. UNC names can make links easier to update when several people will use a linking workbook, because Excel can update links that use UNC names even if users don't have a drive letter mapped to the network share. File names and paths in links Windows have a 255-character limitation on paths. You can't create links to workbooks and worksheets with names that include the characters [ ] and !. Links can only return the first 255 characters in a cell. If you want to link to large amounts of data, first distribute it among several cells on the source worksheet.

Assigning a protection password to a source worksheet or workbook does not prevent users of linking workbooks who don't know the password from updating the links. To make users enter a password to update links, save the source workbook with a password to open (click Save As on the File menu, click General Options on the Tools menu).

http://support.microsoft.com/default.aspx?scid=kb;en-us;328440&Product=x
XL: Description of Link Management and Storage in Excel (June 4, 2003)

Provides useful background on how Excel stores link references.

www.microsoft.com/technet/prodtechnol/office/office2000/tips/exlink2.mspx
Making Links Easier to Maintain

You can update all links in your workbooks automatically, regardless of the type of link and whether the source workbook is open or closed. Click Options on the Tools menu, click the Edit tab, and clear the Ask to update automatic links check box. The next time you open a linking workbook, Excel updates the links without prompting you. This Excel setting affects all workbooks that you open.

3.3.10   Modify a lookup function to return an exact, approximate value.

A *lookup* function provides a means to look up a value in a table, eg, a product code, and return some corresponding value, eg, a price. An *approximate* match means that you are looking for either the exact value or, failing that, the next one to it.

Take VLOOKUP as an example. VLOOKUP searches for a value in the leftmost column of a table. It then returns a value in the same row from a column in the table that you specify. The syntax is:

`VLOOKUP(lookup_value,table_range,col_index_num,range_lookup)`

The fourth argument `range_lookup` is an optional logical value that specifies whether you want VLOOKUP to find an exact match or an approximate match.

If `range_lookup` is omitted or TRUE, an approximate match is returned. If the first value in the table is greater than `lookup_value`, VLOOKUP returns #N/A, otherwise it finds the last row where the value is equal to or not greater than `lookup_value`.

If `range_lookup` is FALSE, VLOOKUP matches the largest value in `table_range` that is less than or equal to `lookup_value`.

As we said in the section on function conventions on page 14, if you omit optional arguments, the program will assume default values. The default behaviour of a function may not be what you expect or want. It is better to explicitly specify option arguments in order to remove any ambiguity.

For example, the last optional argument (match_type) of the MATCH function, eg, `=MATCH(value,array,match_type),` defaults to 1, which requires the list to be sorted in ascending order. If you specify 0, Excel checks *all* the cells in the leftmost column of the array for an exact match.

There follows an example of using exact match in VLOOKUP. The next section on page 99 shows an example of an approximate match.

Example of use of VLOOKUP with exact match.

C15	▼	f_x =VLOOKUP($B15,$B$3:$C$7,2,FALSE)

s3310.xls

	A	B	C	D	E	F
1	Price List					
2		Product Name	Price			
3		Belt	10.99			
4		Light mud	29.50			
5		Hypoallergenic mud	89.00			
6		Sealing cloak large	230.00			
7		Creaming table	234.00			
8						
9	Examples of =VLOOKUP($B11,$B$3:$C$7,2,FALSE)					
10						
11		Aardvark	#N/A			
12		Belt	10.99			
13		Carding comb	#N/A			
14		Light Mud	29.50			
15		Creaming table ⟨!⟩ ▼	#N/A			
16						
17						
18			A value is not available to the formula or function.			

The function is returning the price from column 2 of the table given a name to look up. The fourth argument is FALSE to tell Excel to use an exact match. For that reason, the table did not need to be sorted by Product Name ascending.

a) C11 shows #N/A because *Aardvark* is not in the list.
b) C12 is an exact match for *Belt*.
c) C13 shows #N/A because *Carding comb* is not in the list.
d) C14 is a match; note that the case (capitalisation) of *Mud* and *mud* is ignored.
e) C15 shows #N/A because there is a space after *table* in B15 so the lookup fails.

3.3.10 Check your knowledge (*answers on page 175*)

Open the file **s3errors.xls**. On the sheet *Exact*, correct the errors.

> **3.3.11   Sort a list that is used for an approximate match in a lookup function.**

An *approximate* match is used when you want the formula to look up a table and you do not expect the exact value that you are looking for to be in the table. To do this, the table must be sorted in ascending order of the values in the first column.

The Excel meaning of approximate match is the largest value equal to or **not greater than** the target value. Therefore it does not necessarily return the **nearest** match. To understand how this works, follow this step-by-step description. Take a sorted list, eg, 10,20,30 and look up 19 in this list. Start from the beginning of the sorted list and search for a match for the target value as follows:

a) You find a value less than the target value, eg, 10. Therefore proceed to check the next value. However, if you are already on the last value, stop there and regard that position as an approximate match.

b) Find the target value exactly; the current row is the match. (This does not happen in the current example.)

c) Find a value greater than the target value, eg, 20. Take the previous position (position 1) as the approximate match – even if the current value (20) is closer to the target value (19) than the value (10) in the previous position. If you are on the first position in the table, there is no previous position, so the result is #N/A – 'not available'.

Excel actually uses a binary search algorithm[8] rather than a simple sequential search as described above. Therefore, if the list is unsorted, Excel will seem to return figures at random from the list.

For that reason, always **sort the list** if you want LOOKUP, HLOOKUP, or VLOOKUP to return an **approximate** match.

---

[8] When a list is sorted, you can find data quickly by successively halving the part of list to be searched.
http://en.wikipedia.org/wiki/Binary_search

Example of VLOOKUP with approximate match

C13	▾	f_x	=VLOOKUP($B13,$B$3:$C$7,2)

s3310.xls

	A	B	C	D	E
1	Price List				
2		Product Name	Price		
3		Belt	10.99		
4		Creaming table	234.00		
5		Hypoallergenic mud	89.00		
6		Light mud	29.50		
7		Sealing cloak large	230.00		
8					
9	Examples of =VLOOKUP($B11,$B$3:$C$11,2)				
10					
11		Aardvark	#N/A		
12		Belt	10.99		
13		Carding comb	10.99		
14		Light Mud	29.50		
15		Toasting fork	230.00		

The function is returning the price from column 2 of the table given a name to look up. No fourth argument is supplied, so the default value of TRUE (*approximate match*) is assumed by Excel. It would be clearer to explicitly supply TRUE as a fourth argument rather than relying on this default behaviour.

a) C11 shows #N/A because *Aardvark* is earlier in alphabetical sort order than the first item in the list, *Belt*.

b) C12 is an exact match for *Belt*.

c) C13 also returns the price for the first row in the table because the second row *Creaming table* is later in sort order than *Carding comb*.

d) C14 is an exact match; note that the case of *Mud* and *mud* is ignored.

e) C15 is the last row in the table because *Toasting fork* is later in sort order than the last value in the table.

Tips

- When looking up text values, check carefully for extra spaces in the list values or the target values. These spaces may cause the match to fail.

- Check the value of the offset argument. A common mistake in selecting the position of the return value is to be off by one column or row.

- If you want an exact match, the table does not have to be sorted but you must specify FALSE for the fourth argument. See the example on page 97.

---

http://support.microsoft.com/default.aspx?scid=kb;en-us;181212

Performing a Lookup with Unsorted Data in Excel

LOOKUP requires that the first column of the vector (or the first column or row for the array form) is sorted in ascending order.

If you are looking for an exact match in Microsoft Excel, the first column of a lookup table does not have to be sorted to use the VLOOKUP and HLOOKUP functions. To look for an exact match, specify the fourth argument of VLOOKUP or HLOOKUP as FALSE. If you omit the fourth argument, or specify the argument as TRUE, you must sort the first column of the table.

You can use a combination of the INDEX and MATCH functions to return the same information that a VLOOKUP returns. You need not sort the first column of the table.

=INDEX(Table_Array,MATCH(Lookup_Value,Lookup_Array,0),Col_Num)

3.3.11 Check your knowledge (*answers on page 176*)

Open the file **s3errors.xls**. On the sheet *Approx*, correct the errors.

CATEGORY: 4 Outputs

This comprises two skill sets:

4.1 Appropriate Display

> You may be surprised by what you can find in a spreadsheet once you know the many ways data can be hidden there!

> We describe a common misuse of the ROUND function when a rounded display is intended.

> We show what happens when data is entered as the wrong type.

> We show the different ways that versions of Excel sort tables of data, and you can test your own version.

> We describe common mistakes in filtering data.

4.2 Charts

> We show how to make chart types more meaningful.

Skill set: 4.1 Appropriate Display

4.1.1   Reveal data hidden by formatting.

4.1.1.1   Reveal data hidden by custom formatting

A *custom format* may be used to mask a data value completely. Instead of the usual formatting characters, such as # or 9, literals may be used to display a different value. Usually, when you select a cell you see the real contents on the formula bar. If the cell is also formatted as hidden, the formula bar display is suppressed while the worksheet is protected. The combination of hidden and custom formatting is sufficiently unusual behaviour that most auditing tools will highlight it for investigation.

To find these custom formats, use the menu Format > Cells > Number > Custom, and then scroll down the list carefully looking for characters other than 0 , $, # , ( ).

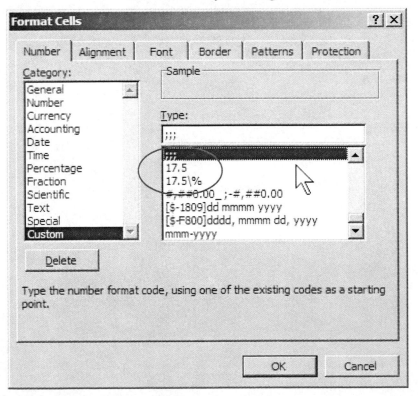

Formats like "17.5" will be shown as literals rather than the underlying data. The three-semicolon format ";;;" suppresses all display because it specifies a blank display for values which are positive; negative; zero; or text.

To find which cells are formatted in this way, use the Edit > Find menu. Ensure the Options are shown. Click the Format button; choose Format from the dropdown menu. If Clear Find Format is enabled, there is a previous format specification that you may wish to clear first. Select the Number > Custom format you wish to check. In the Within box, select Workbook. Then click Find All or Find Next.

To clear a custom format, apply any other cell format you wish, such as General.

To learn more, search Help for 'Create or delete a custom number format'.

4.1.1.2 Reveal data hidden by same font/background colour

When the font colour is the same as the background, the values are hidden from view. If you select the cell you should see the real contents on the formula bar. But if the cell is also formatted as hidden, the formula bar display is suppressed while the worksheet is protected.

To find which cells are formatted in this way, use the Edit > Find menu. In the Within box, select Workbook. Ensure the Options are shown.

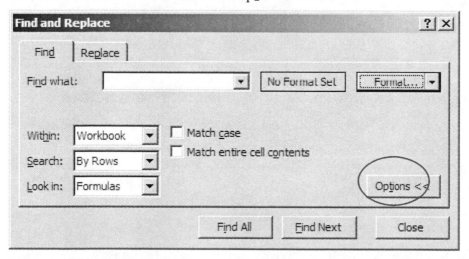

Click the Format button, choose Format from the menu; you may wish to first select Clear Find Format to remove any previous format specification. Select the Font tab and click the Color drop down menu. Select the colour you wish to look for – for example, white text.

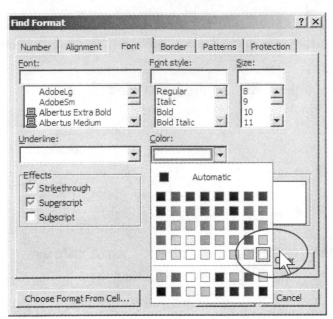

Then click Find All or Find Next as you prefer. To clear a font format, apply the General format. This is an example of white font on white background:

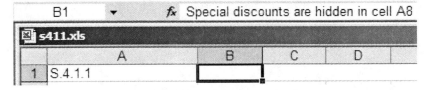

4.1.1.3 Reveal data hidden by suppression of zero values

This is an option in Excel: Tools > Options > View tab > Window options, Zero values. When unselected, zeroes appear as blank. The default setting of Excel is to show zeroes.

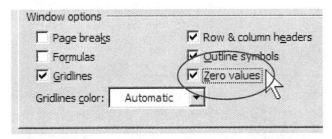

Cell contents may be obscured by overlaid objects

As the worksheet first appears:

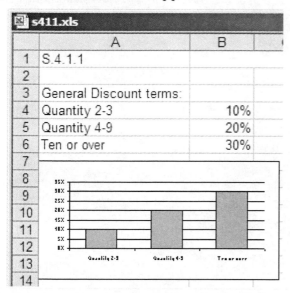

When the chart is moved down:

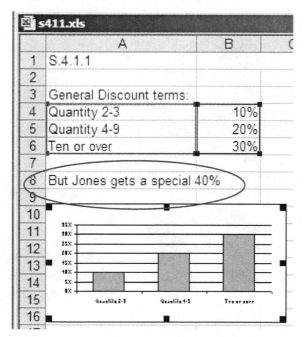

Cell text may overrun under occupied cells

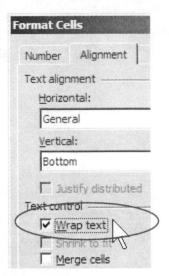

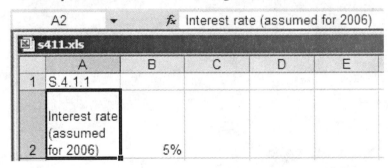

Use Format > Cells > Alignment tab > Wrap text to automatically wrap the text over several lines in the cell. This can avoid hiding important long text entries behind the entry in the next cell to the right.

Reveal all by copying

Section 5.1.3 on page 142 describes a technique to reveal all formulas and data by making a copy of a worksheet without any formatting.

✎ **4.1.1 Check your knowledge (*answers on page 176*)**

Open the file **S4output.xls**[9]. On the sheet *Obscure,* correct the errors.

---

[9] Download the example workbooks from http://www.sysmod.com/sbp

4.1.2	Understand difference between format decimals and ROUND.

Sometimes people reading spreadsheet reports are puzzled when they see percentages not adding up to 100, or rounded totals not agreeing. Don't confuse the ROUND function with a display format that rounds the decimal places.

Do not apply the ROUND function to numbers when a total is required. Instead, format the display while keeping data to full precision. ROUND produces values that are different from those they refer to; formatting only changes the display.

Example

Percentages

Name	Region	Sales	Share	Rounded	Formatted
Homer	MA	63000	25.28%	25%	25%
Graham	NY	100500	40.33%	40%	40%
Alfred	MA	3700	1.48%	1%	1%
Skip	CT	21000	8.43%	8%	8%
Clyde	NJ	61000	24.48%	24%	24%
	TOTAL	249200	100%	98%	100%

- The column **Share** is each sales figure divided by the total sales. It is formatted as percentage to two decimal places. It adds up to 100%.

- The column **Rounded** uses =ROUND(Sales/Total,2), to calculate the percentage with no decimal places. The figures below x.5% will round down, losing up to 0.005 each. It adds up to only 98%.

- The column **Formatted** is the same as **Share** but formatted as percentage to no decimals. It adds up to 100% because the full precision is preserved.

4.1.2 Check your knowledge (*answers on page 177*)

Open the file **S4output.xls**. On the sheet **Round**, correct the errors.

> ### 4.1.3   Correct cell content of incompatible data type such as numbers entered as text.

In this section we describe several ways of accidentally entering a number as text, and how to avoid them. Check for any instances of them in any worksheet you are examining.

Pressing the spacebar instead of pressing Delete

A common mistake by beginners intending to clear the contents of a cell is to enter a space in a cell rather than pressing the Delete key. If that space is referred to directly by another formula, it will produce a #VALUE! error. An error value is easy enough to see but when aggregate functions such as SUM treat non-numeric values as zero, it may not be apparent. A space cell is ignored by COUNT, which only counts numeric cells, but is counted by COUNTA, which counts all non-empty cells.

Entering a non-numeric character in a number

If you enter a currency amount with a currency sign different from your locale[10], Excel will treat the entry as text. So a user in the UK who enters $1.23 or in the US who enters £1.23 will get a text entry, not a numeric value.

`http://catless.ncl.ac.uk/Risks/20.30.html#subj10`
Risks Digest 16 April 1999 From: Ben Bederson Subject: Space character in number causes silent Excel miscalculation Error of US$19,130. 'I had specifically right-justified the column in question earlier. The issue here is that the "19, 130" was interpreted by Excel as text rather than as a number. Since Excel doesn't generate warnings when adding text, but rather interprets it as 0, I had no notification of the problem.'

---

[10] A *locale* is an operating system setting for your Regional and Language Options. See the Control Panel Help for "change number, currency, time, and date settings".

Entering a number into a cell formatted as text

Normally, the only time you want to do this is when you are entering digits that do not represent a quantity. Examples would be a stock code, credit card number, account number, etc.

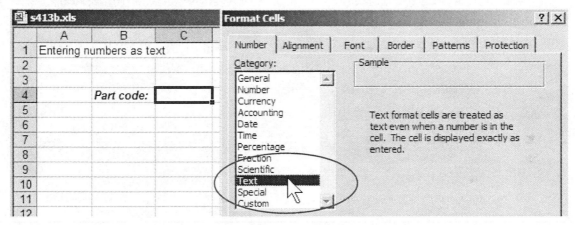

A drawback of this method is that Excel often applies to a cell, in which a formula is being entered, the format of the first cell referenced in the formula. So, if you subsequently create a formula that refers to a text-formatted cell as the first reference, you may be surprised to see the formula itself appearing in the cell. You will need to override Excel's default behaviour by formatting the formula cell yourself. If the first cell referenced is formatted as a date, you may also have to reformat a date arithmetic cell to display a numeric result.

Auditing tools (on page 163) can highlight text cells which look like they should be numeric because they contain only digits and separators such as commas.

Tips

- Where you have numbers unavoidably entered as text, perhaps from an external database, you can use the VALUE() function to convert them to numbers.

- A reference to a cell containing text may show as a zero; this may better be shown using the T() or TRIM() text functions.

- If a credit card number is entered as a number, the 16th digit is dropped by Excel as it only handles 15 digits of precision. When entering long numeric codes that are not numeric values, type an apostrophe ('single quote') first, or pre-format the cells as text.

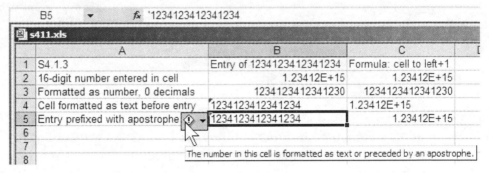

- A logical value of TRUE has the value of 1 when referred to directly, but zero if included in a SUM range.

- A cell containing a number stored as text and right-justified to look like a number is probably a mistake or a deliberate ploy.

- Entering a number into a cell formatted as a date will initially cause confusion. It should be easily recognised, however, and corrected by clearing the format. On the other hand, accidentally including a date in a numeric calculation can be easily overlooked, as the Colorado incident reported below shows.

Risks of entering a date as a number

http://www.ed.gov/about/offices/list/oig/auditreports/a07c0009.doc

2002: Audit Of The Colorado Student Loan Program's Establishment And Use Of Federal And Operating Funds 'We found a $36,131 transfer to the Operating Fund that was not supported. A formula in the spreadsheet picked-up the **date**, 12/02/98, and **interpreted it as a dollar amount**, resulting in an error of $36,131.'

Risks of data type inference

Excel tries to be helpful in inferring what the meaning of data entry may be. It guesses that by SEPT2 you meant September 2nd of the current year; which caused problems to scientists entering genetic data[11] as this report illustrates:

http://www.biomedcentral.com/1471-2105/5/80

Mistaken Identifiers: Gene name errors can be introduced inadvertently when using Excel in bioinformatics. Barry R Zeeberg et al.BMC Bioinformatics, June 2004. When processing microarray data sets, they noticed that some gene names were being changed inadvertently to non-gene names. For example, the text SEPT2 was converted to a date. The problem was default date format conversions and floating-point format conversions in Excel. These conversions are irreversible; the original gene names cannot be recovered.

Examples of Autocomplete are on page 88 and Autocorrect on page 163.

4.1.3 Check your knowledge (*answers on page 177*)

Open the file **S4output.xls**. On the sheet *Datatype*, be sure you understand why the results are as they are.

---

[11] www.eusprig.org/stories.htm#Genetics

4.1.4   Correct a cell range incorrectly sorted by one column.

In older spreadsheet programs, this was more of a risk. Modern spreadsheet software checks first for a data region around the active cell. However, if you have empty rows or columns in the data range, perhaps for spacing or presentation reasons, they break the pattern. As a result, the automatic detection of the database area will come up short. This risk may not be obvious when these empty rows or columns are hidden or out of view in a large table.

This is an example with only two columns selected:

	C	D	E	2C
	First name	Last name	Age	
	Arthur	Smith	22	
	Bertie	Owens	33	
	Carl	Lionheart	24	
	David	Howard	45	
	Edgar	Cabot	34	

Click on the Sort Ascending button on the standard toolbar:

And this is the result:

	C	D	E
	First name	Last name	Age
	Arthur	Cabot	34
	Bertie	Howard	45
	Carl	Lionheart	24
	David	Owens	33
	Edgar	Smith	22

The selected data is sorted by its first selected column, not including column C.

Hidden rows or columns are not sorted. Search <u>H</u>elp for 'Troubleshoot sorting' to learn more.

To correct a mistake immediately after it has been made, you should be able to use UNDO (Ctrl+Z). If not, you may be able to revert to a previously saved backup (see on page 23).

How different versions of Excel sort selected data

For ease of reading the table on the next page, the alert messages that Excel displays are condensed. The table below gives the condensed and full messages:

Auto-select, Sort Dialog	Automatically selects the data without the headers, shows Sort dialog
Alert: 'No list'	'No list was found. Select a single cell within your list, and then click the command again.'
Sort Selection Warning	'Sort Warning: Microsoft Excel found data next to your selection. Since you have not selected this data, it will not be sorted. What do you want to do? (1) Expand the selection (2) Continue with the current selection.'
Alert: 'Not valid'	'The sort reference is not valid. Make sure it's within the data you want to sort, and the first SortBy box isn't the same or blank.'

Differences in Data Sort in Excel versions

The table below describes what Excel (97, 2000, and 2002/03) does when you use either the Data Sort command or the A-Z, Z-A toolbar buttons. The italics show the different behaviour of the versions of Excel.

Selection	Data Sort Command	A/Z and Z/A toolbar buttons
Cell outside table separated by an empty row or column	Alert: 'No list'	Nothing happens. *Excel 2002/3 Alert: 'No List'*
Cell outside the edge of the table, adjacent to the table	Auto-select, Sort Dialog	Automatically selects the data without the headers. Alert: 'Not valid'
A header cell, in the top row of the table	Auto-select, Sort Dialog	Sorts all data by selected column
A cell inside the table data	Auto-select, Sort Dialog	Sorts all data by selected column
Two cells in a row inside the table data	Sort Selection Warning	Nothing happens. *Excel 2002/3: Sort Selection Warning*
A range of cells in a single column inside the table data	Sort Selection Warning	**Sorts selected data with no warning** *Excel 2002/3: Sort Selection Warning*
Cells in a block inside the table data	**Sort Dialog on selected data only, with no header row.**	**Sorts selected data with no warning**
An entire column (click on column letter)	Sort Selection Warning	**Sorts selected data with no warning** *Excel 2002/3: Sort Selection Warning*
Multiple entire columns (click on column letters)	**Sort dialog on selected columns, no warning**	**Sorts selected data with no warning**
Entire row (click on row number)	Sort Selection Warning	Nothing happens apparently. *Excel 2002/3: Sort Selection Warning*
Multiple entire rows (click on row numbers)	**Sort Dialog on selected data only, no warning**	**Sorts selected data on first column with no warning**

www.debating.net/aida/Results/Easters%202002%20Team%20Report.htm

2002: Australasian intervarsity debating association 'The major error in the tabulation was introduced sometime after the draw for round two was announced, but before results from round two had begun to be entered into the tab spreadsheet. The data in the spreadsheet was re-sorted, so that the teams were listed alphabetically, but, mistakenly, not all columns were sorted.'

Tips on database lists

- A spreadsheet does not enforce referential integrity in a database. The user has to build in lookup or validation formulas to check whether, for example, sales item codes entered in an invoice are present in the table of valid product codes.

- Plan ahead. When setting up a table of personal names, rather than putting the full name in one cell put their first name in one cell and their surname in the next cell to the right. It makes sorting cleaner, and you will probably need to sort it someday. If you need to combine them for reporting, you can use the & (concatenation) operator. For example, if B9 contains *Smith* and C9 contains *Jane*, placing in cell D9 the formula =C9&" "&B9 will show *Jane Smith*. Note the use of the space character in quotes to separate the words.

- Place database tables in worksheets separated from calculations. This will ensure that their structure does not become corrupted by insertions and deletions necessary to maintain the calculation formulas.

- Database queries need to be refreshed to be sure they reflect current data.

- Learn how to use Pivot Tables for analysis. It can save a large volume of analysis formulas.

4.1.4 Check your knowledge (*answers on page 178*)

Open the file **S4output.xls**. On the sheet *DataSort*, select columns C and D by selecting the two column letters. Sort the data either by clicking the A-Z button, or using the menu **Data > Sort** and click OK. Observe that column B was not included in the sort. Press Ctrl+Z or use <u>E</u>dit > <u>U</u>ndo to undo the sort. Repeat the experiment this time selecting cells C1 to D15 and note the same outcome. The same behaviour happens in versions of Excel up to 2003.

CATEGORY: 4 Outputs, Skill set: 4.1 Appropriate Display

> **4.1.5   Correct database range in a worksheet to get correct query output.**

In spreadsheet terms, a *database* (or *list*) is a table of data where the first row contains identifying column headings (*field names*). When you add records to a database table, extend the *database range* in your filter command or formulas to include the new row.

When you use the *Data Filter* command, modern spreadsheet software checks around the active cell for a region of data bounded by empty rows and columns and automatically expands the database area. Therefore there should be no blank rows or columns within your list. Nonetheless, check that the ranges for database, criteria, and output all correctly reflect the current data before you publish a report. As query output is not automatically updated, run the query and check before you print.

Use only one list per worksheet, and give it a range name. Separate it from calculations. In this way its structure does not become corrupted by insertions and deletions carried out for other purposes.

How to apply automatically formats and formulas in lists

When you turn on extended formats and formulas, Microsoft Excel automatically formats new data that you type at the end of a list to match the preceding rows. It automatically copies formulas that repeat in every row. To be extended, formats and formulas must appear in at least three of the five list rows preceding the new row. On the Tools menu, click Options, and then click the Edit tab. To format automatically new items to match the rest of the list, select the Extend list formats and formulas check box. Another effect of this setting (what we call the 'Phantom Formula Fixer') is described on page 81.

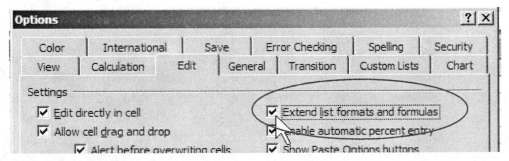

4.1.5 Check your knowledge (*answers on page 178*)

1) Open the file **S4output.xls**. On the sheet *DataFilter*, enter the word **North** in cell F2. Click on cell B1, which is in the list to be filtered. Use the menu command <u>D</u>ata > <u>F</u>ilter > <u>A</u>dvanced and observe the list range is shown as B1:D15. Click OK and the list is filtered in-place showing only the North sales. <u>Click Data > Filter > Show All</u> to show the entire list again.

2) Enter **15-Jan-2004** in cell B16, **North** in C16, and **777** in D16. Click the menu command <u>D</u>ata > <u>F</u>ilter > <u>A</u>dvanced and check whether the <u>L</u>ist range has been automatically expanded to include B1:D16. It should be.

3) Now repeat the experiment with a difference. Close the workbook and do NOT save the changes. Re-open the workbook and repeat Step 2 above. This time, Excel may not automatically extend the list range. So always check!

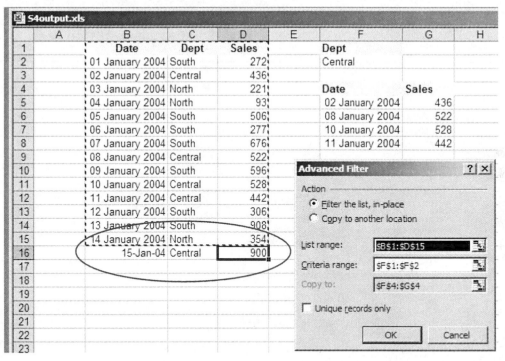

> **4.1.6   Correct database criteria.**

A *criteria* range is a range of cells that specifies what data is to be filtered in a database table. It is easy to make mistakes in Criteria ranges. We give some common problems and their solutions.

How to avoid common mistakes

A space is not empty!

In the following example, no output is appearing. That is because the criterion cell E4 has '**Smith** ' with a trailing space. Stray spaces are often a problem because they are not visible.

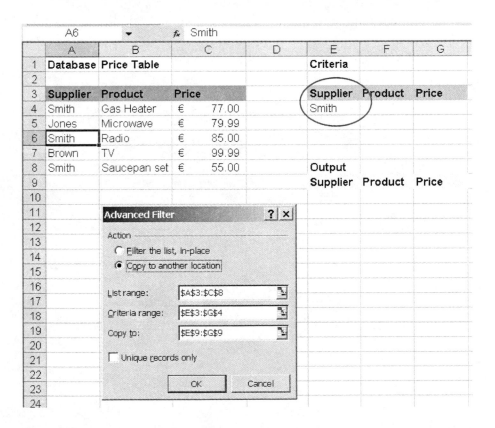

Selecting cell E4 and pressing F2 shows the cursor flashing after the space at the end of the entry in the formula bar:

| E4 | ▾ ✕ ✓ *fx* | Smith | |

S4output.xls

	A	B	C	D	E	F	G
1	Database	Price Table			Criteria		
2							
3	**Supplier**	**Product**	**Price**		**Supplier**	**Product**	**Price**
4	Smith	Gas Heater	€77.00		Smith		
5	Jones	Microwave	€79.99				
6	Smith	Radio	€85.00				
7	Brown	TV	€99.99				
8	Smith	Saucepan set	€55.00		Output		
9					**Supplier**	**Product**	**Price**

Wrong data type

This is where you enter a text value that cannot be found in a column of numeric values, or vice versa.

Too many criteria

If you specify two rows for criteria, and leave one blank, that will match all records.

Mixing OR and AND

The most common confusion is not being sure which way around to put multiple criteria – across a row or down a column?

The *and* rule is that conditions that must all be satisfied at the same time for any one record must be placed across a row. That is, 'it must be *this* and *this* and *this*'.

Example: express 'I want Supplier Smith records where the price is more than 80' as:

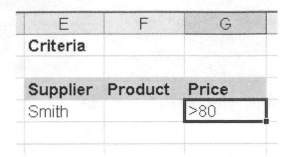

The *or* rule is that if any (or all) of the conditions need be satisfied for any one record, they are placed down a column.

Some confusion may be caused by the use of the word *and* in English in a non-exclusive way to mean what in a spreadsheet would be expressed as *or*. For example, in ordinary speech one might say: 'I want records for the suppliers Smith and Jones'. The way to express this is to ask for any record where the column *Supplier* contains either *Smith* or *Jones*. This needs a criteria range with a heading row and two criteria rows, illustrated here by a dashed outline

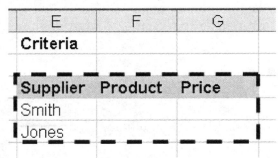

4.1.6 Check your knowledge (*answers on page 178*)

Open the file **S4output.xls**. On the sheet *DataCriteria*, click on cell B1, which is in the list to be filtered. Use the menu command <u>D</u>ata > <u>F</u>ilter > <u>A</u>dvanced and click OK. No records are shown. Why? Click <u>Data > Filter > Show All</u> to show the entire list again.

CATEGORY: 4 Outputs, Skill set: 4.2 Charts

Skill set: 4.2 Charts

4.2.1   Modify chart layout so that all data series are clearly visible.

The *layout* of a chart is the orientation and sequence in which the data series are displayed. You may need to rotate a chart to be sure that taller bars do not hide shorter ones behind them.

In this example, starting with this chart where the series in front hides the rest:

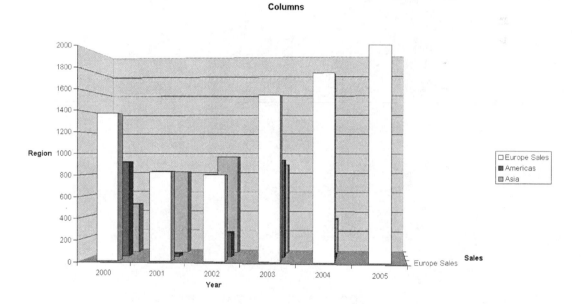

One method is to change the plot order to Europe, Asia, Americas, to reveal the obscured series.

Point to the corner of the chart and the mouse pointer changes to crosshair. Drag the corner handles and rotate the chart until all the points are visible.

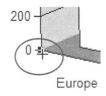

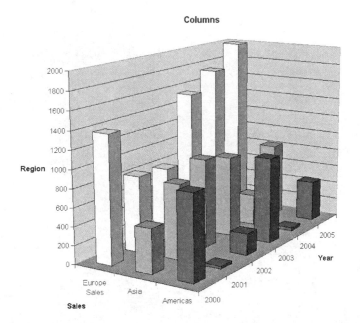

4.2.1 Check your knowledge (*answers on page 178*)

Open the file **S4output.xls**. On the sheet *Chart1*, ensure that all data series are visible in the chart.

4.2.2   Modify the scale of chart axes to clarify chart output.

The *scale* of axes is the range of numbers from the lowest to highest to be charted. Choose scales that represent the data series in a fair manner. You may need to increase the size of a chart to show all the data labels.

Correct the scale and origin of chart axes that obscure the meaning of a chart. Always show the zero point of a chart range unless you have good reasons for doing otherwise that all readers of the chart will understand.

This chart shows a dramatic increase in sales:

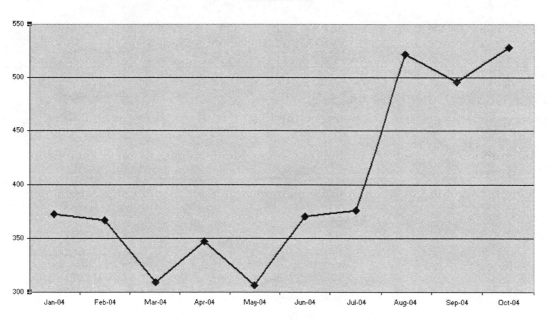

Sales Jan to Oct

It looks less dramatic when the scale is adjusted from a range of 300 to 600 to a range of 0 to 600:

Sales Jan to Oct

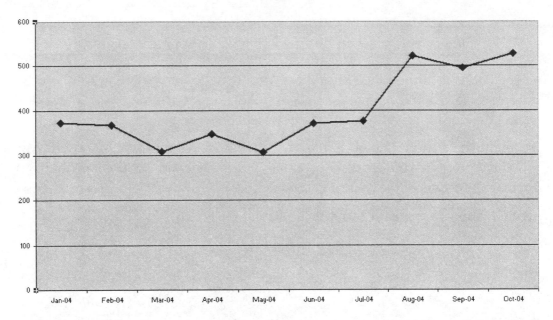

To adjust the vertical scale, point to the *value axis* (on the left), right-click, choose F**o**rmat Axis. On the **Scale** tab, ensure the **Auto** box is checked if you want automatic scaling, or uncheck it and type in the minimum value for the chart to start at:

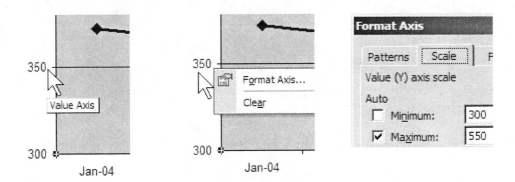

4.2.2 Check your knowledge (*answers on page 178*)

Open the file **S4output.xls**. On the sheet *Chart2*, try changing the scale on the chart.

4.2.3   Modify chart type to clearly express the meaning of data.

Select the appropriate *chart type* to give the clearest presentation of the relationship between data series. Examples are time series for line chart, parts of a whole for pie chart, causally related for X-Y.

A **Time series** is usefully done either with a column chart or a line chart:

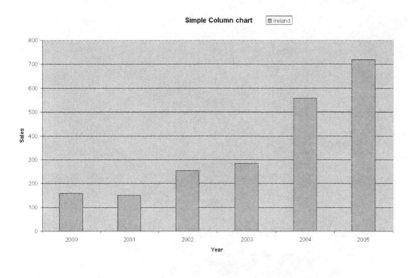

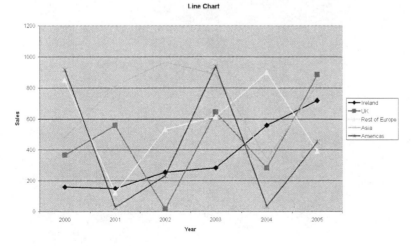

Parts of a whole: For a single series, a pie chart is useful:

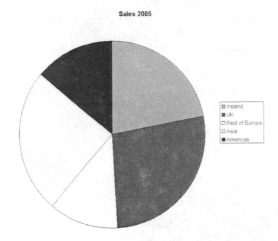

For multiple series, a stack-bar chart may be better:

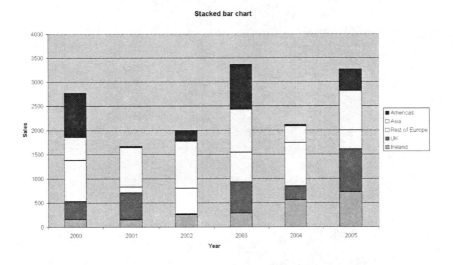

A **Cause**-effect relationship is shown by X-Y or scatter charts, to which trend lines can be added.

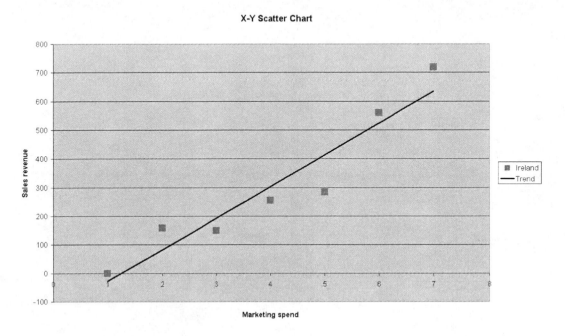

Search your spreadsheet Help to learn the specifics on how to create charts.

4.2.3 Check your knowledge (*answers on page 178*)

Open the file **S4output.xls**. On the sheet *Chart3*, choose a more appropriate representation for the chart.

Blank page for notes

CATEGORY: 5 Review

This comprises two skill sets:

5.1 Testing

5.2 Data Integrity

This section will enable you to answer these key questions:

- Do you have a plan to test your spreadsheet?

- Have you tested your spreadsheet after the last change?

- How do you know you have tested it enough?

We give examples of test cases that indicate how much detail is needed to cover the logic paths in even a simple spreadsheet.

We cover here more examples of how to reveal structure that may be hidden in spreadsheets. In particular, we describe how to inspect formulas and find discrepancies in blocks of formulas.

We cover various techniques for conditional formatting and data validation, with worked examples. These are key skills in developing safer spreadsheets. It assures data quality by either advising or enforcing conditions that must be met by data typed in.

Skill set: 5.1 Testing

5.1.1   Create and run test cases covering all logic paths.

A test plan defines who applies what *test cases* to the spreadsheet, when, and how.

A *test case* is a calculation with a known correct answer and a set of inputs chosen to exercise the spreadsheet. Traditional software testing can validate an application once and it can then safely be left to the users to operate. But testing a spreadsheet once merely gives assurance at a point in time, because its formulas can be changed. Without strict controls on structural and data changes, spreadsheets tend to deteriorate over time. Therefore re-validate a spreadsheet after changes.

Typical input values are those you would expect to be entered. You should know from previous experience what result is expected for this, perhaps from previous documentation or standards.

Extreme values are large negative or positive numbers, or percentages over 100%, values that are below and above those provided to CHOOSE() and LOOKUP() functions, and so on. These values are intended to stress-test the spreadsheet to be sure that it does not give plausible but incorrect answers when the input is wildly different from expected. Include those that are intended to cause an error, in order to show that the spreadsheet handles erroneous conditions properly. If you think that rogue or abnormal data are impossible, be prepared to be surprised how often mistypes can cause these exceptional conditions to happen.

Covering all logic paths means to repeat the tests, with different combinations of input data, so that all conditions are tested in functions such as IF, MAX, MIN, CHOOSE, LOOKUP, etc.

When using *typical input values*, if historical known results are available, they are a good basis for gaining acceptance of the accuracy of the spreadsheet. Do not be satisfied to simply observe that the result 'looks about right'. Just checking that the answers look reasonable or plausible will catch gross errors but not subtle ones. The more risk there is from the answer being incorrect or the narrower your margin for error is, the more carefully you need to check that the answer is exactly correct.

Verify the outputs by calling upon a different pair of eyes. Have an expert with knowledge of that problem domain check the input and output figures.

Printouts can be read more quickly and accurately than computer screens, so they are a good method of final review. On the other hand, readers tire easily and skip repetitive materials.

Examples of test data values

1. A large negative number like -1E100
2. -1, 0, and 1
3. A large positive number like +1E100
4. Just under the lowest expected value
5. The lowest expected value
6. A set of expected values with known results
7. The highest expected value
8. .000000000000001 just above the highest expected value (there are 14 zeroes after the decimal point)
9. A very long number: hold down the 9 key until the input wraps to a second line
10. A space
11. Empty cell
12. A different data type, eg text or logical where number or date is expected. Logical (Boolean) values are either TRUE or FALSE.
13. An error value such as #N/A

Sample payroll spreadsheet test cases

The following is an example of three test cases to exercise the logic paths in the sample payroll tax calculation spreadsheet. The first uses expected values as given in an official document with specified results. The second has lower pay so that *Cumulative Gross Pay To Date* less *Cumulative Std Rate Cut Off Point* cannot be less than 0. The third tests the case when the *Gross Pay* is less than the *Tax Credit* so that the formula for cumulative tax (*Cumulative Tax Due at Std Rate + Cumulative Tax Due at High Rate – Cumulative Tax Credit*) cannot be less than zero.

Test Cases for spreadsheet example specification in section 1.1.1 on page 6

Date of payment	Gross Pay	Cumul Gross Pay to date	Cumul Std Rate Cut off Point	Cumul Tax due at Std rate	Cumul Tax due at High rate	Cumul Tax Credit	Cumul Tax (not less than zero)	Tax deducted this period
Case 1: Official example calculation (Source: http://www.revenue.ie/wnew/employ.pdf)								
10/01/05	€2,400.00	2,400.00	1,644.45	328.89	317.33	123.34	522.88	€522.88
10/02/05	€1,600.00	4,000.00	3,288.89	657.78	298.67	246.68	709.76	€186.88
10/03/05	€2,000.00	6,000.00	4,933.33	986.67	448.00	370.02	1,064.65	€354.88
Case 2: Pay below Cumulative Std Rate Cut Off Point so should pay no tax at high rate.								
10/01/05	€1,600.00	1,600.00	1,644.45	320.00	0.00	123.34	196.66	€196.66
10/02/05	€1,600.00	3,200.00	3,288.89	640.00	0.00	246.68	393.32	€196.66
10/03/05	€2,000.00	5,200.00	4,933.33	986.67	112.00	370.02	728.65	€335.33
Case 3: Pay below Tax Credit, Cumulative tax cannot be less than zero.								
10/01/05	€ 500.00	500.00	1,644.45	100.00	0.00	123.34	0.00	€ -
10/02/05	€ 700.00	1,200.00	3,288.89	240.00	0.00	246.68	0.00	€ -
10/03/05	€ 800.00	2,000.00	4,933.33	400.00	0.00	370.02	29.98	€ 29.98

How to enter an identical test value in all input cells

Simple values like all zeroes, or all ones, are useful because it is easy to calculate expected values. For example, the sum of a column of 1s is the number of rows in the column. If you fill a block of input cells with zeroes and the total is not zero, there may be a hidden number in the formulas.

To enter the same test value in all input cells:

1. Select all the input cells. This is done by selecting the final result cell and then selecting all its precedents at all levels. Excel only selects precedents on the active sheet, so if formulas refer to other sheets you will have to check the other sheets separately.

2. Within those selected precedent cells, select only the constant and blank cells.

3. Type a test value and press Ctrl+Enter to enter that into all the selected cells.

This is an example:

Open the file **Budget.xls**[12]. Select the total cell F11 on the sheet *Forecast*.

Click Edit > Go to > Special, select Precedents, all levels:

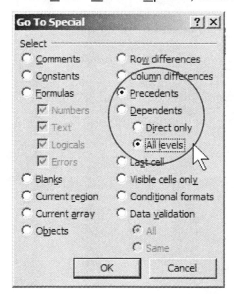

---

[12] Download the example workbooks from http://www.sysmod.com/sbp

Below is what you should see when you click OK. Do not change the selection as we shall be making another selection within this.

B11	▼	*fx* =B4+B5-SUM(B7:B9)

Budget.xls

	A	B	C	D	E	F
1	Forecast					
2		*2006*	*2007*	*2008*	*2009*	*Total*
3	*Sales*					
4	Dept. A	38308	42139	46353	50988	*177787*
5	Dept. B	1000	1000	1000	1000	*4000*
6	*Costs*					
7	Direct costs	4900	5000	5100	5234	*20234*
8	Overheads	18122	21000	19234	18468	*76824*
9	Biennial		10000		10000	*20000*
10						
11	*Profit*	16286	7139	23019	18286	*64729*
12						

Now check whether there are any blank precedents. Click Edit > Go to > Special, select **Blanks**:

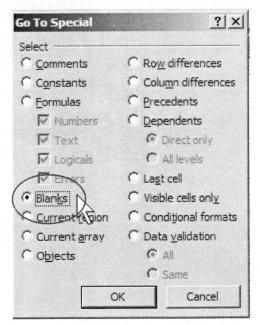

This is what you should see when you click OK:

B9	▼	*fx*			

Budget.xls

	A	B	C	D	E	F
1	Forecast					
2		*2006*	*2007*	*2008*	*2009*	*Total*
3	*Sales*					
4	Dept. A	38308	42139	46353	50988	*177787*
5	Dept. B	1000	1000	1000	1000	*4000*
6	*Costs*					
7	Direct costs	4900	5000	5100	5234	*20234*
8	Overheads	18122	21000	19234	18468	*76824*
9	Biennial		10000		10000	*20000*
10						
11	*Profit*	16286	7139	23019	18286 ✚	*64729*
12						

Only cells B9 and D9 remain selected. We shall enter a zero into these in order to be sure that we have no missing inputs.

Type a zero and press Ctrl+Enter to enter it into the selected cells:

9	Biennial	0	10000	0	10000	*20000*

Now check for numeric precedents. Select cell F11. Click Edit > Go to > Special, select Precedents, all levels, OK. Click Edit > Go to > Special, select Constants.

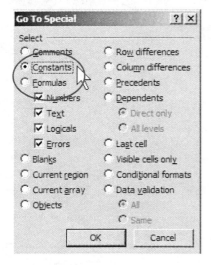

If the formulas refer to text cells, for example in a lookup table, you can select only the constants that are numbers by unchecking Te**x**t, Lo**g**icals, **E**rrors. For this example we will select all the constants. Excel will select only simple constants, not constants that begin with an equals sign, such as =5000 or =2*2500.

This is what you should see when you click OK:

| B5 | | ▼ | | *fx* | 1000 | |

Budget.xls

	A	B	C	D	E	F
1	Forecast					
2		*2006*	*2007*	*2008*	*2009*	*Total*
3	*Sales*					
4	Dept. A	38308	42139	46353	50988	*177787*
5	Dept. B	1000	1000	1000	1000	*4000*
6	*Costs*					
7	Direct costs	4900	5000	5100	5234	*20234*
8	Overheads	18122	21000	19234	18468	*76824*
9	Biennial	0	10000	0	10000	*20000*
10						
11	*Profit*	16286	7139	23019	18286	*64729*

The ranges B5:E5 and B7:E9 are selected. B4:E4 has a formula.

Let's put a zero into all of these so we know we have covered all inputs.

Type a zero and press Ctrl+Enter to enter the value into all the selected cells:

| B5 | | ▼ | | *fx* | 0 | |

Budget.xls

	A	B	C	D	E	F
1	Forecast					
2		*2006*	*2007*	*2008*	*2009*	*Total*
3	*Sales*					
4	Dept. A	38308	42139	46353	50988	*177787*
5	Dept. B	0	0	0	0	*0*
6	*Costs*					
7	Direct costs	0	0	0	0	*0*
8	Overheads	0	0	0	0	*0*
9	Biennial	0	0	0	0	*0*
10						
11	*Profit*	38308	42139	46353	50988	*177787*

Repeat the exercise above on the sheet *Fiddled Forecast*. Try entering values of 0, 1, and 1000 into all the input cells, and check the results. You should that find the figure in E7 is a constant formula, and that the totals in column F have been adjusted. The test with all zeroes should show the fixed amount in F8. The test with all 1000 should show the *1.1 multiplier in F7.

5.1.1 Check your knowledge (*answers on page 179*)

1) Open the file **Wall.xls**[13]. On the sheet *Spec*, create tests based on the specification.

2) Apply these tests on the sheet *Wall1* and report any errors.

3) Apply these tests on the sheet *Wall2* and report any errors.

4) Select all the input cells on *Wall2*, including assumptions, and enter the number 1 in them all. What result should you get?

---

[13] Download the example workbooks from http://www.sysmod.com/sbp

5.1.2   Verify outputs by using a different calculation method.

Putting in two different calculations for the same output is a 'belt and braces' double-check. If you get different answers, you know there is something wrong. See also the section on cross-total checks on page 86. Take this example:

	G5		▼		fx	=SUM(G7:G999)				
	A	B	C	D	E	F	G	H	I	
2					STATE	SUMIF check:	203400			
3					MA	DSUM check:	203400			
4										
5	Database area				Extract area		203400	Note: Update these		
6	NAME	STATE	SALARY		NAME	STATE	SALARY	formulas when there		
7	Homer	MA	64000		Homer	MA	64000	are more than 900		
8	Graham	NY	99100		Alfred	MA	2700	names in the list.		
9	Alfred	MA	2700		Gilles	MA	136700			
10	Skip	CT	21200							
11	Lindy	RI	25500							
12	Gilles	MA	136700							
13	Clyde	NJ	62700							
14										
15										

The range name *Database* is A6:C13, *Criteria* is E2:E3. The SUMIF check in cell G2 is:

```
=SUMIF(B7:B999,$E$3,C7:C999)
```

That calculates the sum of every cell in the range C7 to C999 where the contents of the corresponding cell in B7 to B999 match the value in E3. The DSUM check in cell G3 is:

```
=DSUM(Database,$C$6,Criteria)
```

That means to calculate the sum of every cell in the column headed with the label in C6 (*Salary*), in the records in *Database* that match the *Criteria*.

5.1.2 Check your knowledge (*answers on page 183*)

Open the file **S5test.xls**[14]. On the sheet *DoubleCheck*, create a test to verify the total.

---

[14] Download the example workbooks from http://www.sysmod.com/sbp

CATEGORY: 5 Review, Skill set: 5.1 Testing

5.1.3   Unhide formulas, rows, columns, worksheets.

It is possible to hide from view entire worksheets or rows and columns, or the display of cell formulas in the formula bar.

A reviewer needs to be able to unhide structure in a spreadsheet in order to perform a complete review. Whether or not you are informed of hidden structure, check for it anyway to be sure. You may need to obtain a password as discussed on page 27.

5.1.3.1 Unhide formulas

1) If the workbook is shared, unshare it by using the Tools menu, click Share Workbook, click the Editing tab, and uncheck Allow changes by more than one user

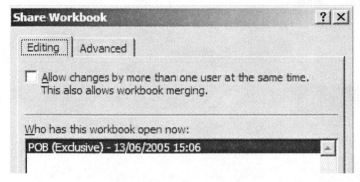

2) If the sheet is protected, use Tools > Protection > Unprotect Sheet.

3) Select the range of cells the formulas of which you want to unhide. On the Format menu, click Cells, and then click the Protection tab. Clear the Hidden check box.

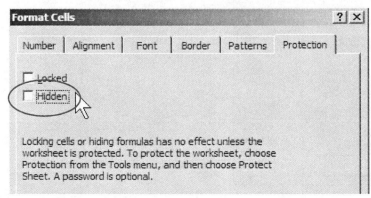

5.1.3.2 Unhide rows or columns

Select a row or column on each side of the hidden rows or columns you want to display. In the example below, click the header of column B and drag right to include column D:

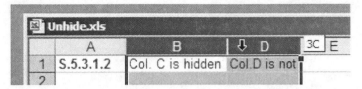

On the F̲ormat menu, point to R̲ow or C̲olumn, and then click Unh̲ide.

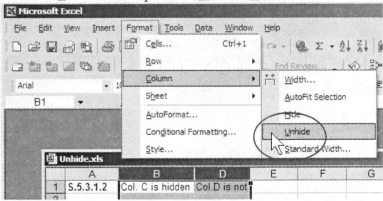

5.1.3.3 Unhide worksheets

On the F̲ormat menu, point to S̲heet, and then click Unh̲ide. In the Unhide sheet box, double-click the name of the hidden sheet you want to display.

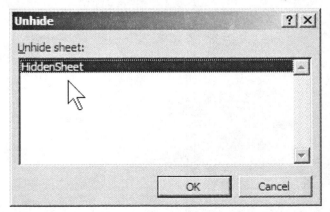

Tips

- If you cannot see the sheet tabs, or the row and column headings, these settings are in <u>T</u>ools > <u>O</u>ptions, View tab, under Window Options.

- If you decide to hide data, that the user does not need to know, make a note in the documentation for the spreadsheet maintainer.

- To display a hidden workbook, on the Window menu, click Unhide. If the Unhide command is unavailable, the workbook does not contain hidden sheets. If both the Rename and Hide commands are unavailable, the workbook is protected from structural changes. In the Unhide workbook box, double-click the name of the hidden workbook you want to display.

- The Unhide command will not show a *Very Hidden* sheet. This sheet property (*xlSheetVeryHidden*) can only be set from VBA code or the VB editor. Developers use this setting so that the user is unaware that a worksheet is there. To access the VBAproject, press Alt+F11. If it is protected by a password, auditing or some navigation tools can reveal very-hidden sheets. Otherwise, click View > Project Explorer, and select the sheet (*HardToGet* in the example below). Click View > Properties Window, scroll down to the end of the properties list, and select the level of visibility required. When finished, click <u>F</u>ile > <u>C</u>lose (shortcut: Ctrl+Q) to close the VBA editor and return to Excel.

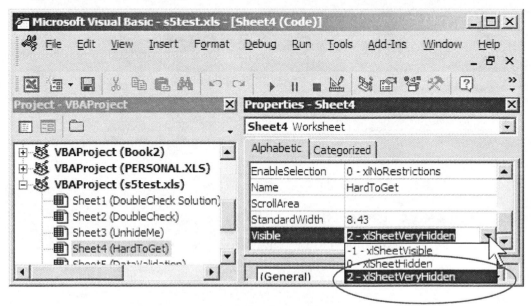

To reveal all in protected worksheets

If the worksheet is protected by a password you can copy its contents to a new worksheet to reveal them. This is true even when you don't have the means to unhide it or to remove formatting (as discussed).

To create a new worksheet to hold the copied data, click Insert Worksheet (shortcut: Shift+F11). If the workbook is protected, create a new workbook by File > New > Blank Workbook (shortcut: Ctrl+N)

To copy an entire worksheet, point to the top left hand corner of the worksheet above 1, and left of A. This is the *select all* button.

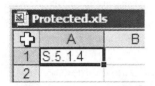

Right-click and select Copy from the drop-down menu. You should see the marquee ('marching ants') around the border of the current sheet.

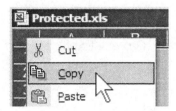

Select a blank worksheet. Select Edit > Paste Special, select Formulas, click OK. Press Escape to cancel the *Select destination* message on the status bar:

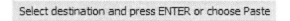
Select destination and press ENTER or choose Paste

5.1.3 Check your knowledge (*answers on page 183*)

1) Open the file **S5test.xls**. Find the hidden worksheets.

2) On the sheet *UnhideMe* find the hidden rows, columns, and cells.

5.1.4   Show all formulas in a worksheet.

There is a convenient way to display formulas without having to view the formula bar for each cell individually.

Menu: Tools > Options > View tab > Window options, Formulas.

Shortcut: press Ctrl+` (back-tick or grave accent). This symbol is usually to the left of the 1 key at the top left of UK and US keyboards. Save time by getting to know the keyboard shortcuts for your application. Appendix B on page 161 gives the most commonly used shortcuts for Excel.

To assist in comparing copied formulas, select Tools > Options > General tab, Settings, R1C1 reference style. This shows formulas in their row & column reference style. This means that the rows are referred to as R1 to R65536 and the columns as C1 to C256. Relative references are R to mean the same row, R[-1] to mean the row above, and R[1] to mean the row below; similarly for relative column references.

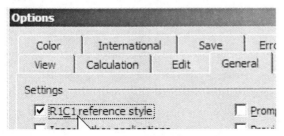

In the sheet *Multiply* in **s5test.xls**, we have a multiplication table where the formula in C4 has been copied across and down:

C4		fx	=$B4*C$3		
A	B	C	D	E	F
1					
2	*Multiplication*	*table*			
3	**Times**	1	2	3	4
4	1	1	2	3	4
5	2	2	4	6	8
6	3	3	6	9	12
7	4	4	8	12	16

This is the table with formulas displayed:

C4	▼	f_x	=$B4*C$3		
	A	B	C	D	E	F
1						
2		Multiplication	table			
3		Times	1	2	3	4
4		1	=$B4*C$3	=$B4*D$3	=$B4*E$3	=$B4*F$3
5		2	=$B5*C$3	=$B5*D$3	=$B5*E$3	=$B5*F$3
6		3	=$B6*C$3	=$B6*D$3	=$B6*E$3	=$B6*F$3
7		4	=$B7*C$3	=$B7*D$3	=$B7*E$3	=$B7*F$3

You still have to read each cell to check if the formula is correct.

Below is the table with the formulas in R1C1 format. This shows more clearly that the underlying formula has been copied without change into all cells.

R4C3	▼	f_x	=RC2*R3C		
	1	2	3	4	5	6
1						
2		Multiplication	table			
3		Times	1	2	3	4
4		1	=RC2*R3C	=RC2*R3C	=RC2*R3C	=RC2*R3C
5		2	=RC2*R3C	=RC2*R3C	=RC2*R3C	=RC2*R3C
6		3	=RC2*R3C	=RC2*R3C	=RC2*R3C	=RC2*R3C
7		4	=RC2*R3C	=RC2*R3C	=RC2*R3C	=RC2*R3C

As an exercise, read that formula; it means 'multiply the value for the current row in column 2 by the value in row 3 for the current column'.

5.1.4 Check your knowledge (*answers on page 183*)

1) Open the file **S5test.xls**. On the sheet *DoubleCheck*:

2) Reveal the formulas.

3) Change the General Settings to R1C1 reference style.

4) Change back from R1C1 style to normal (A1) reference style.

5) Change back from formula view to normal view.

5.1.5   Inspect all formulas in a worksheet.

Inspect is a specific term used in software engineering [Fagan, 1976]. Inspection is a structured process where a team critically examines an item against its specification and user requirements.

To display the formulas on the worksheet use Ctrl+` (backtick), as described on page 143.

For small spreadsheets, use the menu Edit > Go to > Special command to select cells by type. Start with errors, and then check other formulas. With the formulas selected, use the Tab key to move around them. You could format them with a distinctive format pattern to make it easier to review them without being selected. You can then change the format of the cells as you inspect them to make a clear distinction between the cells you have completed and those that remain.

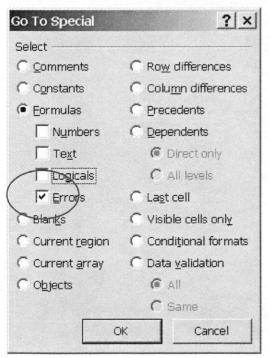

Example of inspecting formulas

Open the file **S5test.xls**. On the sheet *Multiply* enter 4.4 in D5 and =$B6*C$4 in C6. Now find the changes:

	A	B	C	D	E	F
			C3 ▼	*fx* 1		
1						
2		*Multiplication*	*table*			
3		**Times**	1	2	3	4
4		1	1	2	3	4
5		2	2	4	6	8
6		3	3	6	9	12
7		4	4	8	12	16

If you are using Excel 2002 (XP) or later, and have enabled error checking (see Appendix A on page 158), there is a green triangle in the top left of cell C6. Selecting that cell shows an error alert diamond; if you rest the mouse over it you see:

	A	B	C	D	E	F	G	H	I
			C6 ▼	*fx* =$B6*C$4					
1									
2		*Multiplication*	*table*						
3		**Times**	1	2	3	4			
4		1	1	2	3	4			
5		2	2	4	6	8			
6		3	3	6	9	12			
7		4	4	8	12	16			
8			The formula in this cell differs from the formulas in this area of the spreadsheet.						

Press Ctrl+` to display the formulas:

	A	B	C	D	E	F
			C6 ▼	*fx* =$B6*C$4		
1						
2		*Multiplication*	*table*			
3		**Times**	1	2	3	4
4		1	=$B4*C$3	=$B4*D$3	=$B4*E$3	=$B4*F$3
5		2	=$B5*C$3	4.4	=$B5*E$3	=$B5*F$3
6		3	=$B6*C$4	=$B6*D$3	=$B6*E$3	=$B6*F$3
7		4	=$B7*C$3	=$B7*D$3	=$B7*E$3	=$B7*F$3

The constant entry in D5 stands out – yet Excel did not flag it with a green triangle. The change in C6 can also be seen.

How to select cells that differ in a row or column

When you have a group of formulas that all should be the same, you can simplify the task by asking Excel to show you only the differences in that row or column.

Take the previous spreadsheet example and select the cells C4 to F7.

Click Edit > Go to > Special > Row differences:

D5				f_x 4.4		
	A	B	C	D	E	F
1						
2		*Multiplication*	*table*			
3		**Times**	**1**	**2**	**3**	**4**
4		**1**	1	2	3	4
5		**2**	2	4	6	8
6		**3**	3	6	9	12
7		**4**	4	8	12	16

As you can see, cell D5 stands out, and in row 6, D6 to F6 are different from C6.

Select the cells C4 to F7. Click Edit > Go to > Special > Column differences:

D5				f_x 4.4		
	A	B	C	D	E	F
1						
2		*Multiplication*	*table*			
3		**Times**	**1**	**2**	**3**	**4**
4		**1**	1	2	3	4
5		**2**	2	4	6	8
6		**3**	3	6	9	12
7		**4**	4	8	12	16

As you can see, cell D5 still stands out, and now C6 is selected as different from the other columns in row 6.

Ctrl+End moves to the last used cell on the worksheet, in the bottom-most used row of the rightmost used column. If this appears to be an empty area, the cells may be formatted although they have no content. To reset the used range, first select all the cells below the last occupied row and choose Edit > Clear > Formats; then select all the cells to the right of the last occupied column and clear the formats.

For large spreadsheets, you are likely to get tired before you reach the end of the inspection. You would find it easier to use one of the free or commercial tools listed in Appendix C on page 163. Auditing tools are particularly useful in highlighting similar structures in spreadsheets, allowing you to home in quickly on the differences, the exceptions, the breaks in the patterns.

5.1.5 Check your knowledge (*answers on page 184*)

Open the file **S5test.xls**. On the sheet *UnhideMe*, read all the formulas to find any inconsistencies.

CATEGORY: 5 Review, Skill set: 5.2 Data Integrity

Skill set: 5.2 Data Integrity

5.2.1   Use IF function to test if cell contents are within defined parameters.

A formula can show different text in a cell depending on the values in other cells. Use this to provide information about the quality of the data in the spreadsheet. Text may be more clearly readable in back-and-white printouts than colours produced by conditional formatting (on page 150).

Suppose that H10 contains a total across and J10 contains a total down a table of numbers. You can add a check formula like this:

```
=IF(H10=J10, "OK", "Out of balance!")
```

This 'sanity-check' message shows when C8 is more than 1000:

```
=IF(C8>1000,"Too Large?","")
```

This message appears when the current date is later than a date entered into D9:

```
=IF(NOW()>D9,"After review date, check assumptions","")
```

This message in C9 prompts the user that the cell to the right needs a value:

```
=IF(ISNUMBER(D9),"","Enter the ")&"Review date:"
```

For input cells, it's better to put in Data Validation (on page 152) which is more obvious to the user. For calculation result cells, you can still apply Data Validation, but it will not pop up any messages as it does during data entry. You can draw red circles around invalid calculated results by use of the auditing toolbar.

Think of other checks that are applicable in your domain. For example, for bar codes and credit card numbers, test the check digits to catch keystroke transposition errors.

5.2.1 Check your knowledge (*answers on page 184*)

Open the file **S5test.xls**. On the sheet *Budget08*, enter a formula in cell A1 that displays 'Budget for 2008' if the figure in N70 equals that in N69, and displays 'Budget does not balance' otherwise.

5.2.2   Use conditional formatting to highlight specific data attributes.

A *conditional format* is a font, border, or shading pattern that automatically applies to cells if a specified condition is true. Use it to highlight exceptional conditions with colour shading on screen or striped patterns in printouts. For example, you can highlight invoice amounts above 1000 in value, or older than 30 days.

In the following example, we want to highlight cells in a price table where the price is more than 100 euro. Select the cells B4 to B8. On the **Format** menu, click **Conditional Formatting**. To use values in the selected cells as the formatting criteria, under *Condition 1* click *Cell Value Is*, select the comparison phrase (*greater than*), and then type the constant value 100. (To enter a formula start it with an equal sign (=)).

Click the **Format** button, click the **Patterns** tab, and choose an orange colour:

When we click OK, the screen now shows:

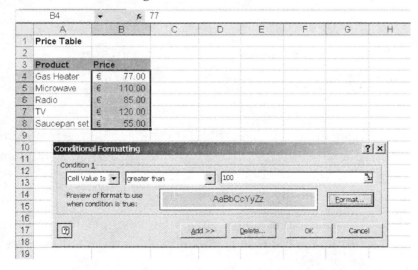

You can specify up to three conditions. To add another condition, in the Conditional Formatting dialogue click Add, and then repeat the steps.

If none of the specified conditions are true, the cells keep their existing formats. If more than one specified condition is true, Microsoft Excel applies only the formats of the first true condition. To learn more, search Help for 'conditional formatting'.

If we wanted the whole product row highlighted, we could use a formula condition. To use a formula as the formatting criterion (to evaluate data or a condition other than the values in selected cells), click *Formula Is* and then enter the formula =$B4>100 that evaluates to a logical value of TRUE or FALSE.

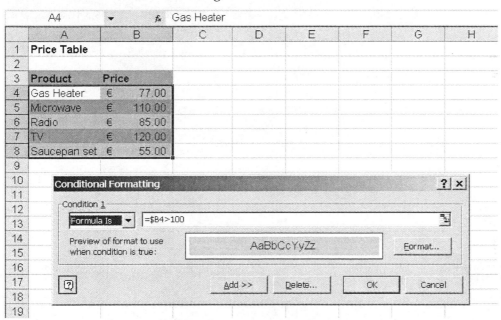

Note that the formula is written with $B4, which means that column B is an absolute reference. When it is applied to every cell in the range, it always refers to column B, while the row is the row of the cell where the conditional format is being applied.

5.2.2 Check your knowledge (*answers on page 184*)

Open the file **S5test.xls**. On the sheet *DoubleCheck*, format the table from row 11 down to highlight rows that have a value of less than 10 entered in column B.

5.2.3   Set data validation criteria.

Control the quality of input data by adding *data validation* to cells. These controls can alert users and where necessary prevent them from entering invalid data. Data validation can also be applied to output (calculation result) cells. It does not prevent the cell from showing invalid results but you can highlight the invalid data with red circles using the Auditing Toolbar of Excel 2000 and later.

In the following example, we want to ensure that the user enters only a positive whole number for the quantity. To avoid doubt about the difference between blank and zero, we shall allow C4 to be blank. If they enter anything, then it must be a whole number greater than zero.

	C8	▼	f_x =C4*C6	
	A	B	C	D
1				
2		Example of data validation		
3				
4		Item quantity:	10	
5				
6		Item price:	€ 12.45	
7				
8		Sales value:	€ 124.50	
9				

The formula in C8 is =C4*C6, to calculate the value from the quantity times the price.

On the **Data** menu, click **Validation**. On the *Settings* tab, choose a criterion from the **Allow** listbox. Depending on what you select, other suboptions appear. For example, if you select Decimal, you can then specify Minimum and Maximum values. The *Input Message* tab specifies a convenient information display that appears only when the cell is selected. The *Error Alert* tab allows you to provide further information and specify whether the user must correct it, whether you ask them to confirm it, or only provide information.

This is the *Settings* tab of the **Data Validation** command:

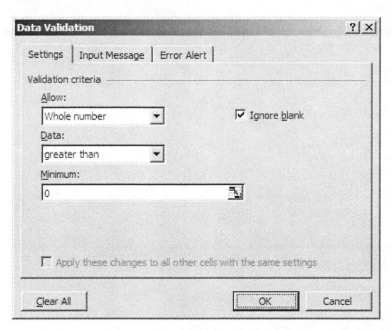

The *Input Message* tab is a tip to the user. There is an option to have it shown in a yellow box as a screen tip when the cell is selected. Whether you do that or not depends on whether the user needs to see the note every time, or whether it may obscure other needed data.

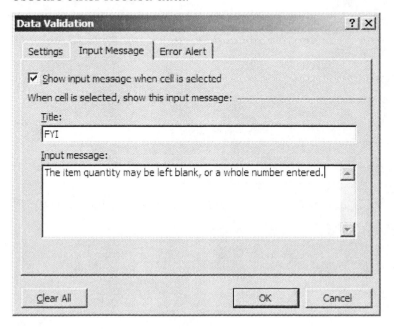

This is how the screen will look after we fill it in and select cell C4. In the example below, the message is moved to the right of its initial position so you could see all the figures.

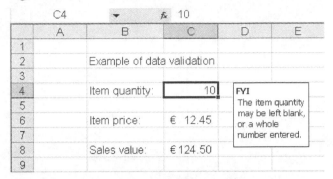

On the final tab, select the Stop style and enter the error alert:

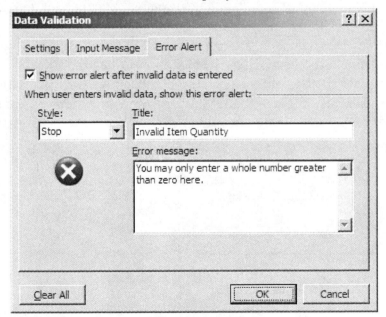

Now try entering 0 or -1 or 2.5 in cell C4 and you get the error message you specified:

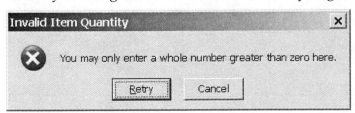

How to use a formula for validation

We want to apply a test to each of the Item Quantity and Item Price cells so that the user is alerted when the combined value is not under 1000. This is the example as it applies to the price. The formula is =$C$8<1000 in the screen shot on the left:

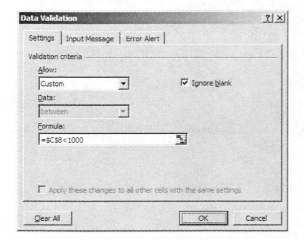
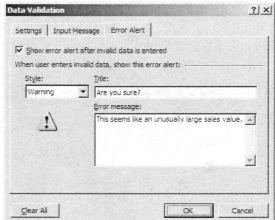

This is an example of how it looks in use:

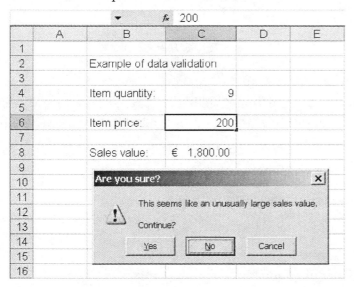

If you want to allow a limit of 1000 and to alert the user only when it goes over that, change the formula from =$C$8<1000 to   =$C$8<=1000

If you want to apply a similar validation to the quantity cell, which already has another validation, you will have to use a formula validation. You have to decide whether you want to stop the user or merely warn them. You cannot have *Stop* applied to one condition (negative quantity) and *Warn* applied to another (large sales value). The formula is:

`=AND($C$4>0,$C$8<1000)`

The AND() function means that all conditions inside the function must be true for it to return *True*.

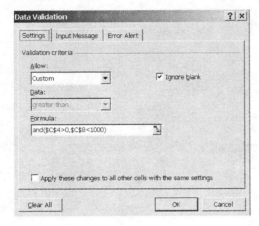

Finding invalid data

If manual recalculation is turned on, uncalculated cells may prevent data from being validated properly. Messages appear only when the user types directly into the cells, not:

- When a user enters data in the cell by copying, pasting, or filling.

- When a formula in the cell calculates a result that isn't valid.

- When a macro enters invalid data in the cell.

To identify cells that contain invalid data regardless of how the data was entered, point to Formula Auditing on the Tools menu, click Show Formula Auditing Toolbar, and then click Circle Invalid Data (described on page 160).

You still have to locate these circled cells, either visually on the sheet or by selecting the cells with validation criteria by the menu Edit > Go to > Special > Data validation. Then press Tab to visit each of the cells and look for red circles.

Option buttons, checkboxes, and list boxes can be used to constrain inputs to predetermined values.

The U.S. Food & Drug Administration (FDA) is responsible for the Code of Federal Regulation no. 21 (21 CFR)[15]. Part 11 of that code deals with electronic records and signatures. They are now issuing warning letters on spreadsheet validation because they are being used in an uncontrolled manner in regulated environments. Examples are given at the website of `http://www.LabCompliance.com`

`http://www.theregister.co.uk/content/67/31298.html` $24M 'Clerical Error'

June 03, 2003 TORONTO (Reuters) - TransAlta Corp. said on Tuesday it will take a $24 million charge to earnings after a bidding snafu landed it more U.S. power transmission hedging contracts than it bargained for, at higher prices than it wanted to pay. As New York ISO rules did not allow for a reversal of the bids, the contracts went ahead. [...] the company's computer spreadsheet contained mismatched bids for the contracts, it said. 'It was literally a cut-and-paste error in an Excel spreadsheet that we did not detect when we did our final sorting and ranking bids prior to submission,' TransAlta chief executive Steve Snyder said in a conference call.

✎ 5.2.3 Check your knowledge (*answers on page 184*)

Open the file **S5test.xls**. On the sheet *DataValidation* apply the validation criteria specified.

---

[15] Title 21: Food and Drugs U.S. Code of Federal Regulations, Part 11: Electronic records and signatures at `http://www.fda.gov/ora/compliance_ref/part11/` and `http://www.fda.gov/cder/guidance/5505dft.pdf` Draft Guidance for Industry on Part 11, Electronic Records, Electronic Signatures--Scope and Application

Appendix A: Microsoft Excel error checking

How to adjust what Excel reports as errors

Excel 2002 and later can flag suspicious formulas with a green triangle in the top corner. The menu item Tools > Options > Error Checking allow you to control this. If you are using an earlier version of Excel, you can get the same checks from auditing tools, see Appendix C on page 163.

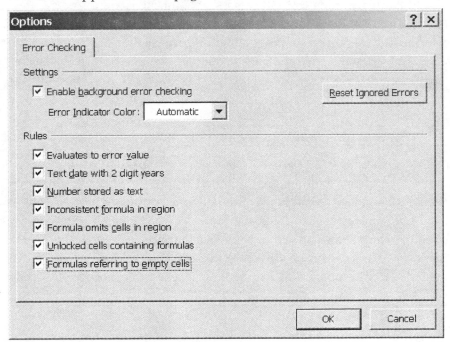

The rules and what they check for are:
- Evaluates to error value
- Text date with 2 digit years
- Number stored as text
- Inconsistent formula in region
- Formula omits cells in region
- Unlocked cells contain formulas
- Formulas refer to empty cells

Correcting formulas

Microsoft Excel has several different tools to help you find and correct problems with formulas. Search <u>Help</u> for 'About correcting formulas' to learn about:
- Watch Window
- Formula error checker
- Formula Auditing toolbar
- Evaluate Formula

Using Excel's Auditing Toolbar

Select Tools, Auditing, Show Auditing Toolbar

The auditing toolbar buttons offer the following functions:

 Formula error checker.
Problems can be reviewed in two ways: one at a time like a spelling checker, or immediately on the worksheet as you work. A triangle appears in the top-left corner of the cell when a problem is found. See *error checking* on page 158.

 Trace Precedents: clicking this button will identify all cells which have been used in the formula of the selected cell. Precedents can be either *direct* or *indirect*:
- *direct* precedents are those referenced directly by the target formula cell;
- *indirect* precedents are those which are used by other formulas prior to those formulas being used by the target formula.

Additional clicks of the button will reveal the first and subsequent levels of indirect precedents.

 Remove Precedent Arrows: this will clear the precedent trace arrows.

 Trace Dependents: this will identify all cells containing formulas which use the data in the selected cell. Like precedents, dependents can be direct or indirect and subsequent clicks will reveal additional levels of dependent cells.

Remove Dependent Arrows: this will clear the dependent trace arrows

Cells can be precedent, dependent or both depending upon their position and use.

 Remove All Arrows: this clears all trace arrows.

 Trace Error: this function can be used to identify possible causes of an error value in a cell.

 New Comment: is a shortcut to the Cell Note dialogue box (Insert, Note…) which allows the user to record comments about a cell. Cells with notes attached contain a red triangle in the top right hand corner.

 Circle Invalid Data: Excel97 or later - this identifies cells that contain values outside the limits set by the user with the Validation command on the Data menu. To see what data restrictions and messages are in effect for a cell, click the circled cell, and then click Validation on the Data menu.

 Clear Validation Circles: Excel97 or later - this clears circles round invalid data.

 Show Watch Window: enables you to watch cell values and formulas in a window even when the cells are out of view.

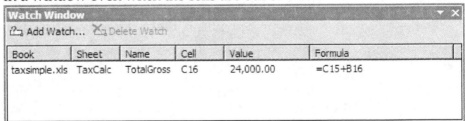

 Evaluate Formula: to see the different parts of a nested formula evaluated in the order the formula is calculated.

Appendix B: MS Excel Keyboard Shortcuts

Navigation and Selection shortcuts

F5	Go To (cell, or special selections)
Shift + navigation key	Extends the selection in the direction chosen
Ctrl+arrow key	Move to the edge of the current data region.
Home	Move to the beginning of the row.
Ctrl+Home	Move to the top left (inside any panes set by Window > Freeze Panes)
Ctrl+End	Move to the last cell on the worksheet, in the bottom-most used row of the rightmost used column.
Ctrl+Backspace	Scroll to display the active cell.
Ctrl+Shift+* (asterisk)	Select the current data region around the active cell. In a PivotTable report, select the entire PivotTable report.
Ctrl+Period	Move clockwise to the next corner of the selected range.
Ctrl+/	Select the array containing the active cell.
Ctrl+\	In a selected row, select the cells that don't match the value in the active cell.
Ctrl+Shift+		In a selected column, select the cells that don't match the value in the active cell.
Ctrl+[(opening bracket)	Select all cells directly referenced by formulas in the selection.
Ctrl+Shift+{ (opening brace)	Select all cells directly or indirectly referenced by formulas in the selection.
Ctrl+] (closing bracket)	Select cells that contain formulas that directly reference the active cell.
Ctrl+Shift+} (closing brace)	Select cells that contain formulas that directly or indirectly reference the active cell.
Alt+; (semicolon)	Select the visible cells in the current selection.
Ctrl (Command) + page down	Activate next sheet
Ctrl (Command)+ page up	Activate previous sheet

For more, search Help for 'Keyboard shortcuts' and click Show All.

Editing shortcut keystrokes

F4 or Ctrl+Y	Repeat the last action.
Ctrl+A	Select All
Ctrl+C	Copy
Ctrl+V	Paste
Ctrl+D	Fill down.
Ctrl+R	Fill to the right.
Ctrl+F3	Define a name.
Ctrl+; (semicolon)	Enter the date.
Ctrl+Shift+: (colon)	Enter the time.
Ctrl+Z	Undo the last action.
Ctrl+Shift+" (quote)	Copy the value from the cell above the active cell.
Ctrl+' (apostrophe)	Copies a formula unchanged from the cell above the active cell.
Ctrl+1	Display the Format Cells dialog box.
Ctrl+Enter	Fill the selected cell range with the current entry.

Other useful keystrokes

Ctrl+` (backquote) Command + backquote	Alternate between displaying cell values and displaying formulas. The single left quote (also called backquote or backtick) may be to the left of the 1 on your keyboard.
F9	Calculate all worksheets in all open workbooks.
Shift+F9	Calculate the active worksheet.
Ctrl+Alt+F9	Calculate all worksheets in all open workbooks, regardless of whether they have changed since the last calculation.
Ctrl+Alt+Shift+F9	Calculates all cells in all open workbooks, including cells not marked as needing to be calculated.
Print Scrn (PrtScr)	Copy a picture of the screen to the Clipboard.
Alt+Print Screen	Copy a picture of the selected window to the Clipboard.
To copy a picture of a range of cells, first select them, then hold down the shift key, click the **Edit** Menu, and click the **Copy Picture** menu item.	

Complete lists of Excel shortcut keys can be found at these web pages:

http://www.ozgrid.com/Excel/ExcelKeyBoardShortcutKeys.htm

http://www.mvps.org/dmcritchie/excel/shortx2k.htm

Appendix C: Websites, software tools

New products arrive every few months. Our current list of web links is at:
`www.sysmod.com/sslinks.htm#auditing`

List of websites as of April 2005:

`www.sysmod.com/scanxls.htm` Collects inventory of spreadsheets and quality metrics. ScanXLS is described on page 192.

`www.hmrc.gov.uk` SpACE from UK Revenue and Customs Audit Dept.

`www.operis.com/oak.htm` Operis Analysis Kit for spreadsheet audit

`www.XLanalyst.co.uk`   XL Analyst from Codematic

`www.SpreadsheetInnovations.com` Spreadsheet Professional audit tool

`www.SpreadsheetAuditing.com` EXChecker inventory and audit

`www.SpreadsheetDetective.com` Southern Cross Spreadsheet Detective

`www.TheModelAnswer.com` Rainbow Analyst free tool for Excel 2000 audit

`www.sheetware.com` XLSpell checker and formula drill-down utility

`www.brandywine-software.com` xlNavigator flow chart of dependencies

`www.codetracer.com` Code Tracer, a spreadsheet visualiser and analyser

`www.kellogg.nwu.edu/faculty/myerson/ftp/addins.htm` Formlist displays formulas of any range.

`groups.yahoo.com/group/eusprig/files/TrafficLights.xla` cell-by-cell Inspection tick-off tool by Phil Bewig

`groups.yahoo.com/group/eusprig/files/CellMaps.xla` Colours cells by type

`www.appspro.com` Rob Bovey's Excel Utilities add-in provides 25 routines for Excel development

`www.robbo.com.au` Navigator Utilities to navigate sheets, ranges, etc.

`www.mastertool.co.uk` Master Tool add-in to handle repetitive tasks

Other useful websites

www.eusprig.org The European Spreadsheet Risk Interest Group website has conference presentations and best practice guides

chacocanyon.com/smm/readings/inspections.shtml Spreadsheet Modeling for Managers: Design Reviews and Spreadsheet Inspections

www.xl-logic.com/pages/design_notes.html Aaron Blood design notes

www.gre.ac.uk/~cd02/EUSPRIG/2001/Butler_2000.htm Risk Assessment for Spreadsheet Developments: Choosing Which Models to Audit by Raymond J Butler, CISA, H. M. Customs and Excise, UK

Sites with Excel tips from Microsoft Valued Professionals (MVPs)

www.appspro.com Rob Bovey

www.oaltd.co.uk Stephen Bullen

www.ozgrid.com Dave Hawley

www.cpearson.com Chip Pearson

PeltierTech.com John Peltier

www.j-walk.com John Walkenbach

msdn.microsoft.com/office Microsoft's resource site

support.microsoft.com/default.aspx?scid=kb;en-us;843504

Microsoft Support description of 75 undiscovered tips about Excel.

Bibliography

A list of books on Excel and spreadsheet applications is maintained at

www.sysmod.com/spreads.htm

Appendix D: 'Check your knowledge' answers

1.1.1   Define spreadsheet specifications

1. What are the risks in omitting a specification for creating a spreadsheet?
   a. The spreadsheet may not meet the user's requirements.
   b. Time, effort, and investment may be wasted.
   c. A wrong solution may cause a financial or reputation loss.

2. What are five key items to include in a specification and which is the most important?
   a. The User Requirements are the most important because they state how the user will judge the correctness of the spreadsheet.
   b. The Purpose – what it is for.
   c. Usability features – designed to help the intended user.
   d. Author – the creator(s) and maintainer(s).
   e. Version History – the evolution of the spreadsheet.

3. What kind of information would you use File Properties for?
   a. Title – the spreadsheet title.
   b. Subject –the topic or area it deals with.
   c. Author – the current maintainer.
   d. Category – eg business area or importance.
   e. Keywords – a list of search terms so that the spreadsheet file can be found by the File Search function in MS Office.
   f. Comments – any other relevant comments.
   g. Manager – the manager responsible for the work area.
   h. Company – name and address.
   i. Custom – any other properties can be added here.

1.1.2   Use cell comments, descriptions

1. What are the risks in omitting comments or supporting text?
   a. The user may enter data that is inappropriate.
   b. The user may misinterpret the meaning of the outputs.

2. When would you use text in cells rather than comments?
   a. When the text needs to be visible at all times rather than only when the user rests the pointer over the cell.

3. List three things you would use comments for.
   a. source(s) of input data;
   b. assumptions made;
   c. user access level.

1.1.3   Make conventions explicit

1. What are the risks in not documenting how functions are used?
   a. The developer or maintainer may use a function inappropriately; for example, applying discounting to the first cash flow in a NPV function when it should be omitted.

2. List three important points about spreadsheet style.
   a. Consistency;
   b. logical data flow;
   c. formatting for meaning rather than decoration

3. Does your organisation have policies on spreadsheet development?
   a. If you don't know, find out!

1.2.1   Make regular secure backups

1. What are the risks in omitting to make backups?
   a. Losing important data.
   b. Extra work to re-create lost knowledge or methods.
   c. Incurring a cost to re-enter lost data.
   d. Loss of business (eg debtors / accounts receivable).
   e. Regulatory fines for non-compliance with retention requirements.
   f. Legal penalties for non-compliance with discovery requests.

1.2.2   Maintain separately saved versions

1.   What are the risks of poor version control and unmanaged changes?

  a.   Using an obsolete version of a spreadsheet

  b.   Not knowing what has changed in a spreadsheet

  c.   Maintainers reverting to previously discarded ideas because the reasons for exclusion were not documented.

  d.   Spiralling costs and time of an out-of-control project

  e.   Abandoning a project that has run out of time or money

  f.   Being unable to revert to a previous working version

1.2.3   Understand the security limitations of passwords

1.   What are the limitations of worksheet password security?

  a.   Worksheet passwords can be broken by software tools.

2.   What are the limitations of workbook password security?

  a.   Workbook passwords may be easily guessable, short, or common words.

1.2.4   Use long mixed passwords

1.   Which are good passwords and which are not good?

  Good passwords are a,c,e,g. Not good are b,d,f,h.

  Password e is rather short at 8 characters.

  Password g is derived from 'rudolph The red-Nosed reindeer…'!

2.1.1   Simplify long formulas, use range names

1.   What are the advantages and disadvantages of breaking long formulas into short ones?

    a.   The advantage is that it makes individual cells easier to read and understand and reduces the risk of error from misreading.

    b.   The disadvantage is that it may be necessary to create hidden rows or columns for intermediate calculations, which may also make the spreadsheet harder to read.

2.   Why are range names better when creating links between workbooks?

    a.   Because they can be used to obtain data from another workbook by name rather than by address. If the source spreadsheet structure is changed, a link by address would still point to the original cells but names are automatically moved with their address by Excel.

2.1.2   Isolate constants

1.   What is the risk in not isolating constants?

    a.   If the value ever has to be changed, it is easy to overlook some of the several places where the value appears.

2.1.3   Identify units of measure and conversion

1.   What is the risk in not identifying units of measurement?

    a.   Running the risk of adding apples and oranges.

2.1.4   Understand use of *Precision as displayed*

1.   What is the risk in using the *Precision as displayed* workbook setting?

    a.   When first applied, precision may be lost in existing data.

    b.   A user may intend to enter data with a larger precision than displayed but they may not notice that decimal places have been truncated.

2.1.5 Manual and automatic calculation

1. What is the risk of the manual calculation setting?

    a. The user may forget to press the F9 key, resulting in the report showing incomplete or out-of-date calculations.

3.1.1   Understand and correct order of precedence

1. The result of -14+10*7 = -14+70 = 56

2. The result of (-14+10)*7 = -4*7 = -28

3.1.2   Remove circular references

1. How can you detect when a workbook has a circular reference?

    a. The word *Circular* appears in the status bar.

2. How can you find a circular reference?

    a. Use the *Circular Reference* toolbar.

3. What may be a circular reference be intentionally used for?

    a. As a means of iterating towards a solution, for example in calculating interest on a balance that itself includes interest paid.

3.1.3   Identify array formulas

1. How would you recognise an array formula?

    a. By the curly brackets (braces) around the formula in the formula bar.

3.2.1   Identify missing input values

1. How would you check whether a formula was missing input values?

    a. Use the precedent tool and check the source cells.

    b. Excel 2002 and later may display a green triangle to warn that 'The formula in this cell refers to a range that has additional numbers adjacent to it', or 'The formula in this cell refers to cells that are currently empty'.

2. Open the file **s3errors.xls** and check for missing inputs on the sheet *Inputs*. Select the region A7:B372 and use <u>E</u>dit > <u>G</u>o To > <u>S</u>pecial > Blan<u>k</u>s. Then use the Tab key to visit each of them in turn. The missing days are Feb 29, Jul 4, and Dec 25. Enter a zero in each of these cells to make the averages agree.

3.2.2   Identify cells with missing dependents

1. How can you check whether a cell has dependents?

To display a tracer arrow to each cell that is dependent on the active cell, click Trace Dependents on the Formula Auditing toolbar.

2. Open the file **s3errors.xls** and check for missing dependents on the sheet *Depends:*

    a. Select the Sales figure in D3 and double click the Trace Dependents button. The arrow only goes to the tax amount, indicating the total does not use the sales figure.

    b. Check the total figure and it is hard coded; change it to =D3+D5.

    c. Double click the Trace Precedents button and note that the tax rate (17.5%) is not referred to.

    d. Check the tax amount and you find that the rate is hard coded; change the formula to =D3*C5. It would be even better to define a range name for the tax rate.

3.2.3   Use information functions: ISERROR, ISNA

1. What is the risk in hiding an error display?

    a. The user may not be aware that an error is there when they need to know.

2. Open the file **s3errors.xls** and use a formula to hide the error on the sheet *Displays.*

A name is in C12 and cell C13 shows the age corresponding to that name. But if you clear C12 or enter a name not in the list, it shows #N/A. It is desired to hide that error display.

The formula currently reads: `=VLOOKUP(C12,B3:C10,2,FALSE)`

    a.   One method is to wrap an IF function around that to test for that value being an error, and if so show blank:

```
=IF(ISERROR(VLOOKUP(C12,B3:C10,2,FALSE)),
    "",VLOOKUP(C12,B3:C10,2,FALSE))
```

    b.   This formula can be made simpler (see 2.2.1) by using the cell B13 to hold the VLOOKUP formula as above, format B13 with Font colour white to make the result invisible, and put in C13:

```
=IF(ISERROR(B13),"",B13)
```

    c.   Another method is to use Format > Conditional formatting, Condition 1 is Formula Is `=ISNA($C$13)`, click Format, and set the font colour to white.

3.2.4   Suppress display of #DIV/0! values

1. What is the risk in displaying a zero rather than #DIV/0?

    a.   Subsequent calculations may give incorrect results rather than showing #DIV/0 to indicate that there is an error earlier in the chain of calculations.

2. Open the file **s3errors.xls**. On the sheet *Div0*, clear the contents of cell C4. Change cell C5 to use a formula to hide the error.

    b.   Change the formula in C5 from `=C3/C4` to `=IF(C4,C3/C4,0)`

3.3.1   Correct relative, absolute and mixed cell references

1. Open the file **s3errors.xls**. On the sheet *AbsRel,* these cell references are in error:

a. C7 contains =C5*B6 which was copied across. The single cell for the price should be an absolute reference $B$6.

b. C10 contains =$C$5*$B$9 which was copied across. The sales units should be referred to in C10 as C5 and then copied to obtain a relative reference.

c. C12 contains =$C7-C$10 which was copied across. The reference to the revenue should have been a relative C7 before copying. The $10 absolute row reference to the cost of sales is harmless as the costs are all in row 10.

2. Here are alternative ways to create a two-way multiplication table where each cell contains the value in the left column times the value in the top row.

a. In cell B3, enter the formula =B$2*$A3 either by typing that in directly or:

   i. Click cell B3 to make it the active cell.

   ii. Type the equals sign, click cell B2 and press F4 twice

   iii. Type the multiplication sign, click cell A3 and press F4 three times

   iv. Press Enter.

b. Then copy the formula in B3 across and down to cell E7. The row reference in the first address is absolute so it will always refer to row 2 whatever row it is copied into. The column reference in the second address is absolute so it will always refer to column A whatever column it is copied into.

c. To copy in one move, first select B3 and click Edit > Copy, or use the Ctrl+C shortcut. Then select all the cells from B3 to E7 and click Edit > Paste, or use the Ctrl+V shortcut.

d. To enter and copy all in one operation, first click in B3 to make it the active cell, select the range B3 to E7, type =B$2*$A3 and press Ctrl+Enter. To learn more about control-key combinations like that, search Help for 'Keyboard shortcuts'.

3.3.2   Identify and correct #error values

Open the file **s3errors.xls**. On the sheet *Errors*, identify and correct all the errors.

1. Row 3 *Agent name* does not appear to an error, read on.

2. Row 5 *Report at* implies a date, B5 contains =-NOW(), it looks like the minus is a mistype, remove it.

3. Row 7 *Credit Card no.* looks as though a long number was entered in B7. B7 contains 1234567890123450. Check the cell format and it is formatted as a number to 2 decimals. Make it General. There is still the possibility that this number is missing a 16th digit because Excel only stores numbers to 15 digit precision. Digits which are not quantities should be entered with a leading apostrophe to make them text.

4. Row 9 *Deposit amount* shows no obvious error, read on.

5. Row 11 *Minimum payment* cell B11 shows #VALUE! because it adds 10 to B9. Select cell B9, press F2 to edit, and you can see a space there that should be deleted. If you are using Excel 2002 or later, you should see an error-checking triangle; point to the yellow alert diamond to see the message 'A value used in the formula is of the wrong data type'.

6. Row 13 *Total so far* cell B13 shows #NAME? The Excel 2002+ screen tip shows 'The formula contains unrecognized text'. The function name total should be SUM. In this case, it was entered in lowercase which is a help.

7. Row 15 *Agent number* cell B15 shows #VALUE! because the third argument is zero. The column index number must be between 1 and the number of columns in the lookup table, two in this case. As the table as no *Agent number* the correction would be to add it to the table or remove the reference in row 15.

    fx =VLOOKUP(B3,Displays!$B$3:$C$10,0)

    VLOOKUP(lookup_value, table_array, **col_index_num**, [range_lookup])

8. Row 16 *Agent Age* cell B16 shows #N/A because the function is looking up the value of B4 which is blank. That should be B3. When you correct it to B3, it shows 45, which is the age corresponding to *David* because there is no *E* in column 1. Type *Edgar* into B3.

9. Row 17 *More info* cell B17 shows #REF! because the third argument is 3. The column index number must be between 1 and the number of columns in the lookup table, two in this case. The correction would be to add the intended third column *More Info* to the table or remove the incorrect formula.

10. In the range A19 to D21, B21 shows #REF! and the formula is =#REF!*0.4. It looks as though some other cell, perhaps C20, was cut and pasted (or dragged and dropped) into cell B20.

11. Row 23 *Logarithm* cell B23 shows #NUM! because the log of zero is invalid.

12. Row 25 *Grand total* cell B25 shows #NULL because the space in the formula =SUM(B3 B23) implies the intersection of the ranges B3 and B23 which is null. It looks like there should be a colon rather than the space between B3 and B23.

3.3.3   Correct inconsistencies in a pattern of formulas

The cells that contain inconsistent formulas are:

- H11:M11

- B17, K17

- N48 is empty

- C67,D67,G67:L67

3.3.4   Correct mistakes in totals caused by inserting, deleting

Open the file **s3errors.xls**. On the sheet *InsRow*, insert a new row at row 11, enter 100 in B11,C11,D11 and then adjust the formulas to obtain the correct totals.

You probably adjusted the SUM formulas to make them sum rows 3 to 11. But did you remember to check the range name *Qtr1* which is used in cell C13 (C14 after the insertion)?

3.3.5   Correct grand totals that double-count subtotals

Open the file **s3errors.xls**. On the sheet *Budget07*, find and correct the double-counted totals.

There is only one, in cell N70.

3.3.6   Correct mismatched cross-check totals

Open the file **s3errors.xls**. On the sheet *Budget08*, correct the cross-check totals at the bottom right.

Cells N48 and C67 are empty.

3.3.7   Correct mistakes created by incorrect use of autosum

The Autosum button does not include headings that are formatted as dates, but does include those that are formatted as numbers. The proposed range C3:C50 includes row 3, the year numbers.

The correct way to use the Autosum toolbar button is to single-click it rather than double-click it; and inspect the range with the border to make sure it is correct.

3.3.8   Replace linking by cell address with linking by range name

This is a worked exercise and the expected outcome is described.

3.3.9   Recognise link references and understand problems caused by changes in linked files.

This is a worked exercise that you should practice yourself.

3.3.10   Modify a lookup function to return an exact, approximate value

Open the file **s3errors.xls**. On the sheet *Exact*, correct the errors.

C11 and C13 can be corrected by adding the product names to the table or changing B11 and B13 to names that are in the table.

C15 can be corrected by removing the space after 'table ' in B15.

3.3.11 Sort a list that is used for an approximate match in a lookup

Open the file **s3errors.xls**. On the sheet *Approx,* correct the errors.

Rows 13 and 14 are both in the table but are showing incorrect prices.

The table needs to be sorted in ascending order by the first column.

C11 can be corrected by adding *Aardvark* to the table or changing B11 and to a name that is in the table.

4.1.1 Reveal data hidden by formatting and other means

Open the file **S4output.xls**. On the sheet *Display,* correct the errors.

a. Cells A1 to C1 are formatted with a black fill colour that hides the text. Correction: Format > Cells > Pattern, No color.

b. Cell D3 has text that is hidden by the three-semicolon custom cell format. Correction: Format the cell as General.

c. The zero in cell C6 is hidden by Tools > Options > View tab, window options, Zero values unchecked. This results in the average function in C8 including the zero and showing 73.33 rather than 110. Correction: clear cell C6 and show zero values.

d. The Tax rate in cell B12 is camouflaged by a custom format that always shows 17.5% regardless of the entry. Correction: change the format to Percentage.

e. Cell D12 has text that is formatted with a white font colour. Correction: remove the font colour.

f. Cells A16 and C16 are obscured by the clip art. Correction: move the picture.

4.1.2   Understand difference between format decimals and ROUND

Open the file **S4output.xls**. On the sheet *Round*, correct the errors.

Correction: change the formulas to calculate the percentage by simply dividing each number by the total and formatting as Percentage to no decimal places.

4.1.3   Correct cell content of incompatible data type such as numbers entered as text

Open the file **S4output.xls**. On the sheet *Datatype*, be sure you understand these effects:

1. Cell B3 contains a space, as shown by the *Data Type* column.
2. Cell B4 is empty. Although the TYPE function considers it a number, the ISBLANK function returns TRUE.
3. Cell B5 contains a date, which Excel stores as a number and uses a cell format to display as a date.
4. The word *true* was enter in Cell B6, giving a logical TRUE.
5. Cell B7 was formatted as text before the number 7 was entered.
6. Cells B8 to B10 were entered with currency symbols; only the euro sign was recognised as currency in this locale.
7. Cell B12 formula =B4+B5+B6+B7+B10 adds up:
   a. B4=blank, treated as zero,
   b. B5=number 1 displayed as a date,
   c. B6=Logical TRUE treated as a 1,
   d. B7=entry of 7 in cell formatted as text, treated as 7,
   e. B10=number 3 displayed in locale as 3 euro,
   f. to get a total of 12.
8. Cell B14 shows a count of 2 because COUNT sees only B5 and B10 as numbers.
9. Cell B16 shows 7 because COUNTA counts the nonblanks – that is, all cells except the blank B4.
10. Cell B18 shows 4 because SUM includes the date number of 1 and the 3 euro amount, but ignores the TRUE.
11. Cell B20 shows 2 because AVERAGE averages the date number of 1 and the 3 euro amount, ignoring the rest.

4.1.4   Correct a cell range incorrectly sorted by one column

Open the file **S4output.xls**. On the sheet *DataSort*, perform the exercise.

4.1.5   Correct database range in a worksheet to get correct query output

Open the file **S4output.xls**. On the sheet *DataFilter*, perform the exercise.

4.1.6   Correct database criteria

Open the file **S4output.xls**. On the sheet *DataCriteria*, click on cell B1, which is in the list to be filtered. Use the menu command <u>D</u>ata > <u>F</u>ilter > <u>A</u>dvanced and click OK. No records are shown. Why?

Because there is a space at the beginning of *Central* in cell F2.

4.2.1   Modify chart layout so that all data series are clearly visible

Open the file **S4output.xls**. On the sheet *Chart1*, ensure that all data series are visible in the chart.

Solution: rotate the chart, or change the chart type, or change the series order, to show the profit in front of the sales.

4.2.2   Modify the scale of chart axes to clarify chart output

Open the file **S4output.xls**. On the sheet *Chart2*, change the scale on the chart.

4.2.3   Modify chart type to clearly express the meaning of data

Open the file **S4output.xls**. On the sheet *Chart3*, choose a more appropriate representation for the chart. Change the chart type from Radar to Column.

5.1.1 Create and run test cases covering all logic paths

Open the file **S5test.xls**. The sheet *Wall2* is protected without a password.

1. On the sheet *Spec*, create tests based on the specification.
    a. The specification does not provide any limits on inputs such as disallowing negative or very large numbers. Most spreadsheet creators would assume that the calculation is simple so the risk of negative or very large answers being missed is low.
    b. You need to calculate some expected results manually first, to have as a basis for comparison with the spreadsheet. For example: (i) A wall 1x1x1 is one cu.ft which should take a half an hour and cost one labour day ($210); plus $7 for brick, total $217; or $10 for lava, total $220. (ii) A wall 3x3x3 is 27 cu.ft which should take 13.5 hours, cost two days ($420); plus $189 for brick, total $609; or $270 for lava, total $690.
    c. There is one conditional test, for the height being more than 5 feet. So three tests should cover just below, at, and above 5 feet to check whether any warning appears about lava rock being unsuitable when the height exceeds 5 feet, and does not appear otherwise.
    d. There is one minimum-size specification that labour is always charged in units of 7 hour days, which may be implemented by a MIN or a ROUND function. So tests should cover just below, at, and above a multiple of 7 hours. Check that at least one day is always charged for, rather than 0 days with 1 hour overtime for a very small wall, eg 1x1x1
    e. The specification mentions overtime as an option but there is no explicit requirement for the spreadsheet to calculate a minimum cost based on whether it is cheaper to work overtime than incur an extra day's cost. This may be covered in a later example.
    f. There is no maximum size. Assume 100 feet for example.
    g. See the following test case table for the input tests.

2. Apply these tests on the sheet *Wall1* and report any errors.
    a. The units are not labelled as feet (although this may be implied and understood by the intended users).
    b. The labour time is labelled as Man days but is actually calculated as hours.
    c. The labour cost is the hours converted to days times $210/day but does not round up to the nearest day;
    d. No overtime is calculated (although this was not an explicit requirement)

e. Work rate (cu.ft./hour), Labour, Brick and Lava rock costs have hard coded constants in the formulas, making changes more difficult than simply changing an input.

f. No warning about the unsuitability of lava rock is shown if a height of more than 5 feet is input.

g. Total cost is shown in two cells without being explicitly labelled, so the reader has to scan around to find out what they refer to – brick and lava rock alternative total costs.

h. All cells are unprotected so any formula can be overwritten.

i. Negative values can be input anywhere.

3. Apply these tests on the sheet *Wall2* and report any errors.
    a. The tests should pass.

4. Enter a 1 in all input cells, including assumptions.
    a. The cost should be 1 for labour, 1 for materials, total 2.00.

Test Cases for Wall.xls spreadsheet. Values are manually calculated to provide expected results to check.

#	Test	Expected behaviour	No OT, Brick	No OT, Lava	With OT, Brick	With OT, Lava
1.	-1 in each Height (H), Length (L), Thickness (T) input cells.	minus results (disallowed)	n/a	n/a	n/a	n/a
2.	-1 in H and L, 1 in T. If entry is allowed, two minuses cancel when multiplied	positive results	n/a	n/a	n/a	n/a
3.	0 in any of H,L,T	Zero results	0	0	0	0
4.	A large positive or negative number like + or - 1E100	Very large, too high for lava.	#####	n/a	####	n/a
5.	H 1, L 1, T 1	1 full day + material cost	217	220	217	220
6.	Height 4.99, L 1, T 1	Lava still OK	244.93	259.90	244.93	259.90
7.	Height 5.00, L 1, T 1	Max ht for lava	245	260	245	260
8.	Height 5.01, L 1, T 1	Too high lava	245.07	N/A	245.07	N/A
9.	Height 2, L 7, T 1	One day exact	308	350	308	350
10.	Height 2, L 7.01, T 1	Two days, 1+ O/T costs less	518.14	560.20	308.74	350.80
11.	Height 2, L 10.5, T 1	Two days, 1+ O/T same cost	567	630	567	630
12.	Height 2, L 10.6, T 1	Two days, 1+ O/T costs more	568.40	632	574.40	638

Appendix D

#	Test	Expected behaviour	No OT, Brick	No OT, Lava	With OT, Brick	With OT, Lava
13.	Height 2, L 14, T 1	Two days exactly	616	700	616	700
14.	Height 10, L 100, T 10	Assumed Maximum	220150	N/A	220600	N/A
15.	A space in any of H, L, T	Invalid	#VALUE!	#VALUE!	#VALUE!	#VALUE!
16.	Empty any of H, L, T	treated as zero	0	0	0	0
17.	TRUE or FALSE in any of H,L,T (Excel treats TRUE as the value 1)	Should be disallowed.	N/A	N/A	N/A	N/A
18.	Text in H,L,T	Invalid	#VALUE!	#VALUE!	#VALUE!	#VALUE!
19.	Date in H,L,T	Treated as number	N/A	N/A	N/A	N/A
20.	An error value such as #N/A	propagated	N/A	N/A	N/A	N/A

5.1.2   Verify outputs by using a different calculation method

Open the file **S5test.xls**. On the sheet *DoubleCheck*, create a test to verify the total.

Solution: Unhide the sheet *DoubleCheck Solution* to see three ways to check this. The best is SUMIF because it checks for an exact match with the currency code, and so excludes any approximate matches. Another check is to add the exact match argument (FALSE), as shown below, to the VLOOKUP function. Invalid currency codes would then return #N/A which would then reflect in the total.

```
VLOOKUP(C11,$C$2:$D$4,2,FALSE)
```

5.1.3   Unhide formulas, rows, columns, worksheets

1.   Open the file **S5test**.xls. Find the hidden worksheets.

   a)   **Format > Sheet > Unhide** will show you the sheet *UnhideMe* and *DoubleCheck Solution* which is the answer to 5.1.2 above.

   b)   The Visual Basic Editor (Alt+F11) will show you the sheet *HardToGet*. This is already illustrated in the text.

2.   On the sheet *UnhideMe* find the hidden rows, columns, and cells.

   a)   Row 6 and column H are hidden.

   b)   The row totals in column I are hidden. Unprotect the sheet – there is no password – to reveal the formulas, which include the hidden column H.

5.1.4   Show all formulas in a worksheet

Open the file **S5test.xls**. On the sheet *DoubleCheck*:

1.   Reveal the formulas by using Menu: <u>T</u>ools > <u>O</u>ptions > View tab > Window options, check Fo<u>r</u>mulas; or press Ctrl+`

2.   Change the General Settings to R1C1 reference style using: <u>T</u>ools > <u>O</u>ptions > General tab, Settings, check R1<u>C</u>1 reference style.

3.   Change back from R1C1 style to A1 style by unchecking the R1C1 option.

4.   Change back from formula view to normal view by pressing Ctrl+` again.

5.1.5   Inspect all formulas in a worksheet

1. Open the file S5test.**xls**. On the sheet *UnhideMe* read all the formulas and find any inconsistencies. You need to know both sections above on how to unhide sheets and how to reveal formulas.

2. You should find that the formulas in E9 and F9 omit some rows. The formulas in this row are inconsistent and it would be better to clean them up by replacing them by a SUM.

5.2.1   Use IF function to test if cell contents are within defined parameters

The formula should be

```
=IF(N70=N69,"Budget for 2008","Budget does not balance")
```

5.2.2   Use conditional formatting to highlight specific data attributes

Open the file **S5test.xls**. On the sheet *DoubleCheck*, format the table from row 11 down to highlight rows that have a value of less than 10 entered in column B.

Solution: Select the cells from A11 to E57. On the Format menu, click Conditional Formatting. In *Condition 1* select 'Formula Is'. In the formula box, type =$B11<10. Click Format. Select the Patterns tab. Select the yellow highlight and click OK. Finally click OK to close the Conditional Formatting dialog.

You should see rows 13,36,39,55, and 57 highlighted.

5.2.3   Set data validation criteria

Open the file **S5test.xls**. On the sheet *DataValidation* apply the validation criteria specified. They are:

1. Allow only whole numbers less than 1 million

    a. Allow: *Whole number*; Data: *less than*; Maximum: *1000000*

2. Allow only positive whole numbers here, blank not allowed.

    a. Allow: *Whole number*; Data: *greater than*; Minimum: *0*; uncheck **'Ignore blank'**.

3. Allow only non-negative numbers, with an input message saying 'Only numbers allowed, not negative'

    a. Allow: *Decimal*; Data: *greater than or equal to*; <u>M</u>inimum: *0*; Input message *Only numbers allowed, not negative.*

4. Allow only either of *apple* or *orange*

    a. Allow: *List*; Source: *apple,orange*. Check '<u>I</u>n-cell dropdown'

5. Allow only date entry. If a date is entered before 1 Jul 2005 show a warning 'This is before Jul 1', but allow the entry.

    a. Allow: *Date*; Data: *greater than or equal to*; <u>S</u>tart Date: *01-July-2005*;

    b. Error Alert style: *Warning*; Error message: This is before *Jul 1,2005*

6. Display an information alert 'Outside working hours' if a time is entered outside 09:00 to 17:00

    a. Allow: *Time*; Data: *between*; Start time: *09:00:00*; End time: *17:00:00*;

    b. Error Alert style: *Information*; Title: *Time Check*; Error message: *Outside working hours.*

7. Do not allow more than ten characters of text if nonblank and say so in the error message.

    a. Allow: *Text length*; Data: *less than or equal to*; Maximum: *10*

    b. Error Alert style: *Stop*; Error message: *must be less than ten characters, or blank.*

About the Author

Patrick O'Beirne BSc, MA, FICS

Patrick is a senior software consultant, trainer, and speaker with a particular interest in spreadsheet quality training, audit, and model review. His company is Systems Modelling Limited, http://www.sysmod.com

Chair 2004-2005 of the European Spreadsheet Risks Interest Group, a director of the Informatics Development Institute, and an Expert Advisor to the European Commission. A certified TickIT ISO9000 auditor, he promotes software development process improvement using the Personal Software Process. He is a frequent speaker at international conferences and the author of 'Managing the Euro in Information Systems' (Addison Wesley, 1999).

European Spreadsheet Risks Interest Group: www.eusprig.org

Informatics Development Institute: www.InformaticsDevelopmentInstitute.net

Fellow of the Irish Computer Society: www.ics.ie/pob.shtml

Would you like to know more?

Patrick O'Beirne provides training for best practice and accelerated productivity, and expert consultancy in spreadsheet modelling, testing, and auditing.

Get a confidential look into spreadsheet issues

In-company consulting provides you with a confidential examination of your most important spreadsheets. Patrick can fast-track you to understanding how and where good spreadsheets have gone bad, and help draw up a training plan to bring other spreadsheet creators and users up to speed.

SCANXLS - Spreadsheet Files Inventory, risk analysis

ScanXLS is a spreadsheet that assists you in IT audit compliance projects related to internal controls on risks in end user development of spreadsheet models. It produces an inventory of your spreadsheets, originally developed for Y2K and Euro conversion projects. It has now been enhanced with complexity, links and error metrics to address concerns in Sarbanes-Oxley (SOX) 404 audits.

Purpose

ScanXLS gives you data for these fundamental questions:

- What spreadsheets do we have where on the network?
- Who is the responsible owner/user/developer?
- How big are they, how complex, have they errors?
- What dependencies/links exist between them?
- Has a spreadsheet changed from an authorized/validated version?

What it does

It scans any given directory and below and obtains a list of all the .XLS files. You then select some or all of these, and it opens each one in turn read-only and reports on some file properties, attributes, the presence of unusual features or settings that may represent a risk or are prone to human error, Excel's error checking summaries, a list of other workbooks that it depends on through links, and a scoring on how 'problematic' it may be. SCANXLS can also compare two workbooks to check whether their formulas and/or values are identical.

How to buy it

A demonstration version is available that merely lists files; it does not perform the detailed scan or workbook comparison. You can buy online at:

http://www.sysmod.com/scanxls.htm

Systems Publishing Order Form

Yes, I want more copies …. Send me:

___ Spreadsheet Check+Control book, price each €29.95

The following table shows Priority Mail shipping cost prices in euro as at Sep 1, 2005. Prices are subject to change without notice because of postage cost increases. The current price list and online ordering form is at http://www.SystemsPublishing.com

Destination:	Ireland	UK & Europe	Rest of World
Post & packaging cost for first book	4.00	6.00	8.00
Up to 3 more books on the same order, each	2.00	3.00	4.00
For orders of more than four books, please contact us for a quotation.			

Post or fax your name, address, postcode, telephone, email, and credit card details including expiration date and security code at the back to:
Systems Publishing,
Suite #2, Villa Alba,
Tara Hill, Gorey,
Co. Wexford, IRELAND
Tel: +353 (0)55 22294
Fax: +353 (0)55 22165

Reader offer

Is your copy more than a year old? Or so used that it is torn and dog-eared? Update or freshen up the book with our special upgrade offer. Just send us the front cover of the book with this order form and take a massive 20% discount per copy on the prices above! We'll send you the brand-new, most up-to-date edition.

Web: http://www.SystemsPublishing.com/

Email: SBP@SystemsPublishing.com

Printed in Ireland by Gemini International Ltd